The True Story of a Ge

Midwife
of Borneo

WENDY GREY ROGERSON
and BARBARA FOX

First published in Great Britain in 2018

Society for Promoting Christian Knowledge
36 Causton Street
London SW1P 4ST
www.spck.org.uk

British Library Cataloguing-in-Publication Data
A catalogue record for this book is available from the British Library

ISBN 978–0–281–08030–4
eBook ISBN 978–0–281–08031–1

Typeset by Geethik
First printed in Great Britain by Jellyfish Print Solutions
Subsequently digitally printed in Great Britain

eBook by Geethik

Produced on paper from sustainable forests

Contents

List of photographs — vii

Historical background — x

Main characters — xii

Wendy in North Borneo — xviii

List of abbreviations — xx

1 The longhouse: October to November 1959 — 1

2 'Who will go for us?' November to December 1959 — 14

3 A hut and a jamban: December 1959 to April 1960 — 24

4 The operating theatre: May 1960 — 43

5 Travels with Arnold: May to June 1960 — 52

6 Rags and riches: June to July 1960 — 63

7 A hard chair and a bucket: July to August 1960 — 81

8 The mission cat: September to December 1960 — 93

9 A schoolboy surgeon: December 1960 to May 1961 — 108

10 The first ice: May to June 1961 — 126

11 Travels with my mother: June to September 1961 — 140

12 An intruder: September to October 1961 — 160

13 A view of the hills: October to December 1961   179

14 A maze of rivers: December 1961 to
   February 1962   196

15 Signals: February to March 1962   207

16 Perfect days: March to May 1962   219

17 Wild horses: May to June 1962   229

18 Endings and beginnings: June to
   October 1962   238

Afterword   255

Glossary of Malay and Dusun words   261

Boats used by Wendy   263

Acknowledgements   264

Photographs

Wendy climbs the notched steps to a longhouse   6

Newspaper reports back home   9

Wendy, her parents and her brother Joe,
    Amble, 1943   15

Wendy's friend, the census chief Lawrence Jones   25

Frank, Bishop Wong and Joan on their way to
    Tongud   32

The house made of bamboo, bark and palm leaves
    that Wendy and Joan shared   35

Baptism at Tongud, with Arnold Puntang,
    Frank Lomax and boatman, Majang, holding
    candles in a bag   38

Wendy visits a patient receiving traditional medicine
    from local women, who sit under a palm-leaf
    shelter   44

Wendy calls Sandakan via the radio in Arnold's
    house   47

Journey to Telupid: Wendy in a *perhau*,
    with *Bintang Epiphany* behind   58

Wendy holds a clinic and gives healthcare advice
    during her travels   61

Wendy helps Ulor take his first walk outdoors,
    watched by his family   67

Wendy house: the living room, with furniture
    made by Andrew Kiri   71

Wendy operates on Nalang, who had been bitten
    by a wild pig   77

Sister Christina reads to her novices   82

A letter from home 90

The Dusun house at Puru-Tawai 98

A welcome break: Wendy and Joan relax on one of
their holidays 109

Wendy diagnoses diseases from stool and sputum
specimens 115

Wendy, Arnold (in hat) and schoolchildren with
mission boat *Malaikat* and *Malaikat Raphael*,
the ambulance *jungkung* 118

Imitation game: schoolboys copy Wendy in a play
for Tamu 123

Samuel assists Wendy with a patient in the
dispensary 124

Rasina and her son, Tering 137

Wendy is accompanied by her mother, Elsie Grey,
on a visit, and for her daily bath 143

Larnia and Samuel with their baby son, Philip 144

Work and play: children from the mission school,
Tongud 147

Wendy and her patient Simin, before and after her
treatment for TB 160

Newly shod: schoolboys are helped with their
first shoes 174

Tongud schoolgirls: Kamsiah, Helena, Fatimah
and Lily 176

Wendy and Samuel (with hat) are taken to visit
the sick by schoolboy boatmen and share the
story of the Nativity 191

Juga is carried along the path from the river to the
dispensary 192

Time to relax: Wendy on the beach with Sheila
and Flo, and with Andrew, Joan and Arnold
celebrating a birthday in Tongud 202

Mission to serve: Joan, her brother John, Frank,
  Arnold, Bishop Wong, Julius and Wendy   210
Arnold teases a boy with a lump of ice   213
'I'm gonna wash that man right outa my hair!' –
  Wendy and Gay at the bathing spot   245
Wendy walks across a tree trunk to visit a patient,
  while carriers bring medicines in *bongans*   246
Rosemary and Arnold Puntang visit Wendy in
  Durham in 1991   257
Wendy and Arnold meet Lily (holding Wendy's hand)
  and her family in 2003   259

Historical background

Borneo, the third largest island in the world, lies on the equator in south-east Asia, roughly midway in a line between the southern coast of China and the north coast of Australia.

From the late 1800s until just after the Second World War, the state of North Borneo – along with Sarawak and Brunei – was a British protectorate, its main attraction lying in the timber resources in its vast rainforest interior. During the war, it was invaded by the Japanese and most of its towns were heavily bombed, Sandakan being so badly damaged that it lost its status as the capital of North Borneo, the administration shifting to Jesselton (today renamed Kota Kinabalu).

When Wendy arrived in 1959, North Borneo and Sarawak had become British colonies, each headed by a governor. The land was divided into residencies and sub-divided into

North Borneo at the time of Wendy's mission

districts, which were run by district officers. These colonial administrators all crop up throughout Wendy's tale.

In the year following Wendy's 1962 departure, North Borneo (now named Sabah) and Sarawak became part of the new independent country of Malaysia, its other eleven states lying to the west on the Malay peninsula. Between them, Sabah and Sarawak cover about a quarter of the land area of Borneo; the rest of the island is shared with a constituent part of Indonesia and the tiny but oil- and gas-rich sovereign state of Brunei, which takes up about 1 per cent of the island.

The Dusun people to whom Wendy ministered in the interior are today known as Kadazan-Dusun, owing to similarities between the two ethnic groups, and form the largest ethnic group in Sabah.

The currency used at the time of Wendy's stay was the Malaya and British North Borneo dollar. One British pound was the equivalent of 8.57 dollars (60 Malaya dollars to seven British pounds).

The word 'jungle', which was in common use when Wendy was in Borneo, is held by some today to be pejorative. Although the word 'rainforest' is more commonly used today, it does not accurately describe the low-lying, thick vegetation that made navigation through it so difficult on Wendy's expeditions, and so the word 'jungle' is used in the text, as Wendy used it in her diaries.

Main characters

Some names have been changed.

Barbara Beaumont	Teacher at St Monica's School, Sandakan
Father Briggs	Anglican priest, Sandakan and Jesselton
John Brummell	Australian principal of St Michael's Secondary School, Sandakan
John Burder	Forestry officer
Father Burn	Rector of All Saints' Church, Jesselton
Dr Cameron	Doctor, Sandakan
Dr Christiansen	Doctor, Sandakan and Jesselton
Sister Christina	Leader of convent CJGS, Sandakan
Dr Clapham	Doctor, Jesselton
Nigel Cornwall	Bishop of Borneo (1949–62)
Dalila	Medicine woman, Tongud
David	Pupil, Tongud
Jean Durrant	Australian teacher at St Monica's School, Sandakan
Ederiss	Former pupil, now assistant teacher, Tongud

David Fielding	District Officer (colonial government post), Tambunan
Sister Florence	Principal of St Monica's School, Sandakan
Dr Fozdar	Surgeon, Jesselton and Sandakan
Dr Galea	Doctor, Sandakan
Gay	American Peace Corps volunteer
Novice Ginyam	Novice, CJGS convent, Sandakan
Governor Goode	Governor of British North Borneo (1959–63)
Lady Goode	Wife of Governor Goode
Joan Goodricke	Australian teacher at mission school, Tongud
John Goodricke	Brother of Joan Goodricke; volunteer at mission, Tongud
OT Harun	Headman, Tongud
Helena	Daughter of the Towkay; pupil and Wendy's assistant, Tongud
Beryl Hobby	SPG nurse, Bunuk (Sarawak)
Noel Hudson	Bishop of Labuan and Sarawak (1932–37); Bishop of Newcastle (1941–57)
Mr Hunt	District Officer (colonial government post), Sandakan
David Hutchinson	Agricultural officer
John Iceton	Dentist
Dr Cyril Innes	Doctor, Sandakan
Lawrence Jones	Census chief, Sarawak and North Borneo

Julius	Filipino teacher at mission school, Tongud
Ray Kelly	Manager of Rivers Estate timber camp, River Kinabatangan
Andrew Kiri	Catechist; founder of Tongud mission
Kutarp	Son of patient Wendy attends while working with Gwynnedd Nicholl, Padawan (Sarawak)
Larnia	Wife of Wendy's assistant Samuel
Lily	Pupil at mission school, Tongud
Frank Lomax	Rector of St Michael's Church, Sandakan (1950–62); founder of North Borneo Interior Mission
Irene Lomax	Wife of Frank Lomax
Majang	Boatman, member of Tongud mission
Flo Martin	Principal of St Agnes' School, Jesselton
Bill Meijer	Dutch forestry officer, Sandakan
Sheila Merryweather	Teacher at St Monica's School, Sandakan
Dorothy Meyer	Friend of Wendy, Sandakan
Tony Meyer	Husband of Dorothy Meyer
Peggy Miles	Secretary to Bishop Wong, Jesselton
Robert Mills	British Army captain and surveyor, Sandakan
Muhammad	Father of Wendy's patient, Farouk

Gwynnedd Nicholl	SPG nurse, Padawan (Sarawak)
(The) Panglima	Tribal chief, Tongud
Anthony Perry	Provost of St Thomas's Cathedral, Kuching
Arnold Puntang	Anglican priest from Sarawak; founder of Tongud mission
Rosemary Puntang	Teacher at mission school, Tongud; wife of Arnold
Rasina	Young woman, Tongud
Rhoda	Wendy's aunt
Mr Roberts	Assistant District Officer (colonial government post), Lamag
Samuel	Wendy's assistant in Tongud dispensary
Bruce Sandilands	Government surveyor and motivator to Frank Lomax, Sandakan
Siew Mann	Chinese student-teacher, Tongud
Simin	Wendy's patient
Simon	Former pupil and apprentice boatman, Tongud
Arthur Stally	Rector of St Michael's Church, Sandakan (1962–65)
Elsie Stephenson	Nurse and Wendy's mentor; Director of Nursing Studies at University of Edinburgh
Dr Sychta	German ENT doctor, Sandakan
Tanguran	Son of OT Harun; temporary assistant to Wendy in dispensary

Angelita Ticobay	Filipino nurse; wife of Father Ticobay, Telupid
Father Val Ticobay	Filipino priest; husband of Angelita, Telupid
(The) Towkay	Father of Helena; owner of the kedai (shop), Tongud
Ulor	Wendy's patient, the first on whom she operates in Tongud
Miss Waites	Colony matron, Jesselton
Peter Warner	Surveyor, Sandakan
Dr Christopher Willis	Owner of Christian Book Room clinic, Sandakan
Martin Wilson	Student on Voluntary Service Overseas
Bishop Wong	Assistant Bishop of Borneo; Bishop of Jesselton (1962–65)
Keith Wookey	The Resident (colonial government post), Sandakan

This book is dedicated to Arnold Puntang and Frank Lomax,
and everyone I met in Borneo
Wendy Grey Rogerson

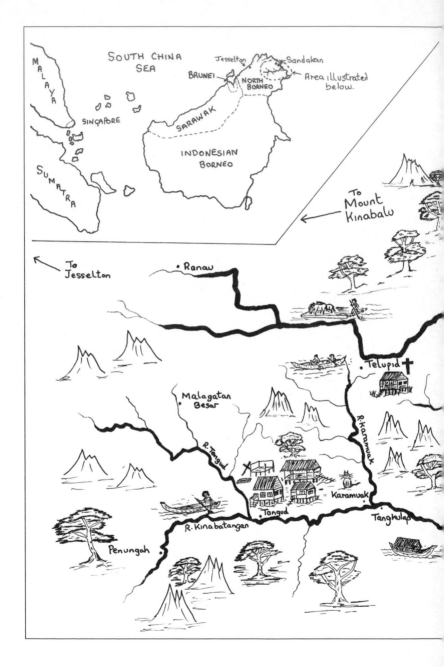

Abbreviations

CJGS	Companions of Jesus the Good Shepherd
NBIM	North Borneo Interior Mission (founded by Frank Lomax)
SPCK	Society for Promoting Christian Knowledge
SPG	Society for the Propagation of the Gospel in Foreign Parts (in Wendy's time)
USPG	United Society Partners in the Gospel (since 2016)

1

The longhouse

October to November 1959

As I came out of the trees towards the mountain edge, I saw for the first time the way ahead of me. A wooden bridge crossed the chasm. It had been constructed from a log, about eight inches wide, but unlike most bridges there was neither barrier nor handrail to prevent those using it from toppling over the edge. Far below, the river twisted and gushed in the still-falling rain. Looking at the bridge, I couldn't help thinking that it had been built by and for the local people, the Dayaks – people far smaller and lighter than me and most Westerners. People with smaller feet than my size fives. People who didn't give a second thought to walking over ravines where one slip might mean plunging hundreds of feet because, in this remote part of Borneo, there was no other way to travel from one village to another.

I had been in Borneo for ten days and had not been expecting things to be easy. Extreme heat and humidity, a new diet, alarmingly large insects: these I had been prepared for. But had I really thought I would be putting myself in such danger? Was I really dedicated enough to risk life and limb in order to nurse people who had no medical care? I watched Gwynnedd striking out ahead of me, took a deep breath and followed her.

Gwynnedd was a nurse, who, like me, had chosen to take her skills to this south-east Asian island. I was staying with her in Padawan, about 50 miles from Kuching, capital of what was then the British Crown Colony of Sarawak, to learn from her before being sent off on my own, and we had already become great friends. It had been something of an adventure to reach Padawan itself, travelling in a Land Rover along a new road cut through the dense tropical vegetation, on which we had, at various points, been stuck in the mud, towed through a river, pushed by a bulldozer and, most dangerously of all – when a fallen tree blocked our route – gone round a mountain bend on just two wheels. I had been thankful when we got out to walk the last part of the journey.

It was Sunday 1 November 1959 – All Saints' Day – and it had begun innocently enough. Gwynnedd and I had just finished breakfast and were planning to spend the day seeing patients in the clinic when a messenger arrived, wet and hungry after a five-hour walk, to say that the father of Kutarp, a trainee at Padawan's government-sponsored school, had fallen from a tree in his village and broken his leg.

Gwynnedd sprang into action and started to clear our breakfast things away. 'We need to go to him. There's no time to waste. We need to get there before nightfall.'

Intrigued as I was, I decided not to ask her what might befall us if we failed to complete our trek in daylight, as I feared the answer might involve getting lost in the forest and wild animals. As I grabbed a light change of clothes, I tried instead to focus on the poor man, who I knew must be in terrible pain, having as yet received no medical treatment.

The messenger carried our equipment and 14-year-old Kutarp, who also accompanied us, carried our supplies – a hunk of bread, a tin of meat and a bottle of orange squash. I could see that he was anxious about his father and my heart ached for him.

The day was already very hot and humid and it wasn't long before we were all dripping with sweat and horribly sticky. As we walked, Gwynnedd pointed out farms of hill *padi* (rice that is planted on land rather than in water) along with fields of tapioca and rubber gardens: all part of the government scheme to make better use of the land. After about 90 minutes we were relieved to reach a store, where the Chinese owner gave us cool drinks.

Feeling refreshed, we set off again. The landscape was different now, the wide open spaces of Padawan replaced by jungle. Mountains that had seemed a long way in the distance when we set off now loomed right before us, and I realized that we were heading straight for them. We began to climb, scrambling up steep slopes, often on all fours, and sometimes finding the descents, though less exerting, even more precarious. We waded through streams and crossed wide rivers over bamboo bridges. When we were so hot and weary I wondered whether I could carry on, we lay down in the water in our clothes.

'Can't we stay here all day?' I pleaded, as Gwynnedd laughed at me and said we needed to get moving.

The next part of the journey involved wading for 20 minutes through thigh-deep water, which was more strenuous than I could have imagined.

Coming up on to the bank I saw the messenger, who was leading the way, stiffen and then suddenly lunge forward. It was all over before I knew what was happening, and as we caught up with him we realized the danger we had been in. A giant king cobra had risen in front of him, poised to attack, and in a split second, he had killed it with his *parang*, a heavy metal sword about 18 inches long which every Dayak man and boy carries around his waist in a sheath made from tree bark.

I looked at Gwynnedd. She just shrugged. 'A good job we weren't in front. I think I would have been frozen to the spot.'

Seeing the look on my face, she added, 'Snakes don't look for confrontation, Wendy. We probably disturbed him from a snooze, the poor devil.'

Just when I thought I was too hot to walk another step, it began to rain heavily. The ground underneath grew muddy and we ended up on our backsides several times, but I don't think any rain had ever felt more welcome.

'Ahhh!' I said, tilting my face to it and closing my eyes. I laughed to myself, too, knowing that I had never knowingly greeted a shower in my native north-east England in this way.

I've always loved singing, and feeling happier now, I started one of my old Girl Guide songs.

It's never any trouble just to S-M-I-L-E
It's never any trouble just to S-M-I-L-E
Whenever you're in trouble
It will vanish like a bubble
If you only take the trouble just to
S-M-I-L-E

Gwynnedd was soon joining in with me, and I taught her some other songs as we carried on our way.

Up and up we went. We sometimes lost sight of the messenger, but Kutarp would be waiting for us to make sure we were on the right track. If it weren't for the fact that Gwynnedd had been to our destination before, or that our messenger and Kutarp were from the *kampong* (village), I would have thought we were lost on several occasions, for I could not believe that anyone would choose to live in such a remote place, nor one that involved such death-defying acts to reach it.

Gwynnedd told me that Kutarp and his family lived in a longhouse, a typical home in this part of Borneo, where a whole community might live together under one roof.

'When I first came to Padawan, people were calling me out to their kampongs all the time,' she said. 'I would turn up after a long trek and realize their complaint was quite minor and they could have made the journey themselves. You can imagine how frustrating that was. Now they are starting to come to the dispensary if they can, and it means I can treat more people.'

The bridge that filled me with such dread turned out to be the first of many, each one no less terrifying than the last. We crossed other ravines and climbed steep slopes using logs with notches carved into them for hands and feet to grip. Well, I was going to be fit at the end of this trip, I thought. That's if I survived it . . .

The longhouse appeared out of nowhere, tucked away near the top of the mountain, and quite hidden from view until we were almost right in front of it. It was a giant wooden house, raised on stilts about ten feet from the ground, too large to see in its entirety. I gazed at it. I had not expected anything so imposing, yet so fragile too, looking as if a strong wind might lift it up and carry it away.

I asked Kutarp – who was learning English at the government-sponsored school as well as being taught farming, carpentry and other skills – why his people had chosen such a spot to live. He replied that their grandfathers, who had been headhunters, had intended the house to be hidden from their enemies.

'Well, they certainly did a good job, Kutarp,' I said, still scarcely able to believe what I was seeing.

While at first glance the longhouse made me think of treehouses from the adventure stories of my childhood, the smell as we approached turned my stomach, and quickly dispelled any thoughts of Enid Blyton. The ground underneath the house, where animals wandered, was a mire of pig, hen and – I suspected – human excreta. To make matters worse, in order to reach the living accommodation we had to climb another notched log, which rose out of this stinking mess. As it was still raining and the wood looked slippery, I prayed I wouldn't lose my grip and land in it.

I was relieved to reach the verandah safely, whereupon a group of people gathered round us. Gwynnedd greeted them and introduced me, and I used the opportunity to practise my Malay. This provoked an outbreak of chatter, and suddenly everyone's eyes were on me. I wondered if I had made a faux pas in speaking Malay when their local language was Dayak, but it turned out there was another reason for their reaction.

'They thought you were a boy, Wendy, with your shorts and cropped hair,' Gwynnedd said. 'But when you started speaking they realized their mistake.'

Wendy climbs the notched steps to a longhouse

I couldn't help laughing and, pleased with my reaction, the people joined in, while continuing to stare. Gwynnedd had already told me that before her first visit, some of them had never met a white woman, and that during my stay in Borneo it wouldn't be uncommon for me to come across people who had never seen a white person of either sex before.

When the laughter had subsided, Gwynnedd spoke in Dayak. A few people responded, and some of them pointed inside the building, shaking their heads as they did so.

Something was wrong. I could see on Gwynnedd's face a flicker of disappointment, but it passed quickly. 'Our patient's house has been *pantang*-ed,' she said to me.

When I looked blank, she explained that the witch doctor was at work and no one was allowed to enter or leave his home for 24 hours after the accident.

I was horrified. We had come all this way, risking our lives in the process. We had put thoughts of our patient before anything else, mindful of the agonies he might be feeling. Were we now going to sit back and let the witch doctor tell us what to do?

'But we have to see him now. Surely someone can speak to the witch doctor and explain?'

Gwynnedd touched my arm. 'It's not our place to interfere, Wendy. But we can see him first thing in the morning. Let's go and get changed and have something to eat.'

I wondered how she could sound so calm about it. I looked at Kutarp, who was equally powerless to intervene. He gave me a thin smile, but I could see that he was upset.

The people showed us to a room we could use. It was a relief to peel off my filthy, dripping clothes and change into a clean blouse and sarong, and to remove my boots and socks and go barefoot. The room had an open fire in one corner but no chimney, the smoke eventually escaping through the doorway, which was also the only means of light.

Having not eaten since breakfast, our bread, which we toasted and spread with the meat and washed down with the squash, was as good as any feast.

All the time we were being watched by pairs of curious eyes. Gwynnedd had warned me that in a longhouse I could have no inhibitions. This was communal living at its most basic and I would have to forget Western notions of privacy. As I squatted on the verandah, which was made of split bamboo slats, all my bodily waste would provide nourishment for the animals living beneath.

I learned that about 300 people lived in this longhouse, and while that seemed an incredible number, I could see that the building lived up to its name and was far more extensive than it had appeared from the ground. Divided between living quarters for individual families and larger communal spaces, it was built entirely of wood and bound together with rattan – which comes from the Malay word *rotan*. The thought struck me again that the whole edifice, built on a slope, with its roof of palm leaves and walls of split bamboo, seemed both a miracle of engineering and terribly insubstantial at the same time.

'Someone I knew fell through a rotten bit of floor on her first visit to a longhouse,' said Gwynnedd cheerfully.

Thinking back to some of the bridges we had crossed earlier, I mused that it was hardly surprising that I had yet to see a Dayak who was overweight!

As we ate, one of the men we had spoken to earlier came back to tell us that they had appealed to the witch doctor to let us see the injured man, but he had refused. Even the headman, who had now joined us – and would later kill a chicken for our evening meal – was powerless to intervene, though he was as worried about the patient as we were.

There was nothing to do but sit on the floor and chat to our hosts, Gwynnedd conversing in Dayak and me making

'Jungle girl' to get £400 a year from Jesmond

SIXTY people in a Newcastle suburb have pledged themselves to give money every week to support a former city girl now working as a missionary nurse in the Borneo jungle.

Already they have promised a total of £400 a year.

The missionary is Miss Wendy Grey, daughter of the Rev. J. M. Grey, Vicar of Healey, near Riding Mill.

Until a year ago, she worked in the Jesmond area, and was a member of the congregation at St. George's Parish Church, Osborne Road.

Half-crowns

Since she left England, parishioners have been raising money to help to equip her dispensary at Tongud, a pioneer mission station in the interior of Borneo.

Now an idea first put forward by the Vicar of St. George's, the Rev. H. Graham Piercy, has led 60 of his parishioners to pledge a weekly half-crown for the Tongud.

"At a meeting of our parochial church council I mentioned almost casually that if 80 people would give half-a-crown each week it would come to £200 a year," Mr. Piercy said last night.

At first hand

A woman church councillor who heard Mr. Piercy's remark decided to act immediately and form the Tongud 80.

In a month 60 people had pledged a total of £400 a year —and they hope to get at least 20 more in the scheme.

"The money is urgently needed. A church has to be built at Tongud, the dispensary needs to grow into a hospital, and a doctor ought to be provided," said Mr. Piercy.

Next Sunday parishioners will hear first-hand news of Miss Grey and her work.

The preacher at all the services will be Canon Frank Lomax, a missionary in Sundakan, Borneo.

From the city to the jungle

— MISS WENDY GREY
A job in Borneo

Today, the story of...

THE GREAT ADVENTURE

The girl with a faith that surmounts jungle perils

THE amazing adventure story we tell today is of Wendy Grey, the Tyneside missionary. Wendy does not know the story is being told—she is thousands of miles away in the steaming jungles of Borneo. Nor would the film please her, for she is modest, unassuming and does not regard her adventures in any heroic way. But it is a story which is infinitely worth telling.

SMOOTH green lawns, interspersed with plots of carefully-pruned rose trees, surround the spacious grey stone vicarage. In the background is a tiny church with a modest tower and woods where the birds chatter undisturbed. The peace is perfect.

On Sunday the vicar's wife serves home-made cakes and girdle scones for tea. The vicar pours tea from a silver teapot.

Both are hoping that tomorrow will bring a batch of air-letters.

For their only daughter is far away from home. Possibly she will be speeding Sunday in her own bamboo home at the Mission of the Epiphany in Tongud, North Borneo, having run of something out of a tin for tea; she may be trekking through the jungle jenuts with a party of natives carrying an infirm

By MOIRA RUTHERFORD

Duchess's School at Alnwick, and is remembered by her schoolmates as a rather reserved girl—not likely to set the world on fire with her adventures.

After training as a nurse

IT'S a long, arduous journey through jungle tracks and down swollen rivers to the nearest medical station. And every jungle counts to the native on the stretcher with third degree burns. But Wendy Grey, seen with her native stretcher party, won the battle against time, just as she has overcome many other crises in the heart of North Borneo.

Wendy's jungle journeys are all in day's work

AROUND ABOUT

THE thought of spending the night in an unexplored jungle with snakes crawling around outside is enough to make many a girl shudder. But for Miss Wendy Grey, a former Newcastle health visitor, such horror is all in a day's work.

For Wendy left the native village of Healey (near Riding Mill, where her father, the Rev. J. M. Grey, is vicar) to become a missionary in Borneo. She has been there about one year now and this month there is an account of her latest exploits in "The Lantern," magazine of St. George's, Jesmond.

Wendy, aged 26, is a former hospital nurse. Since she arrived in Borneo she has had strange—then tickled adventures.

She has been attacked by a king cobra, had a clash with a witch doctor and helped with the rescue of a runaway baby-bear.

This week she tells of an adventure that nearly cost her her own life.

WENDY GREY — a recent photograph from Borneo. Below, Wendy operating on a native suffering from a leg bite.

Canoe trip

AND so this missionary girl went to the nearest medical station to collect medicine. But as she set out on the first leg of the journey she saw the jungle animals before going.

that the leg can come out of hospital after the operation.

Nurse got 'welcome' from witch-doctor

A FORMER Newcastle health visitor will be travelling 200 miles by steamer and dug-out canoe along a Borneo river infested with killer fish.

She is 26-year-old Miss Wendy Grey, who will be making the journey with a young Australian schoolmistress.

They are going to the most isolated mission post in east-ern—and they will be the first two white people ever to reach it.

Since arriving in Borneo as a missionary three months ago, Miss Grey, an ex-hospital nurse, has been attacked by a king cobra, had a clash with a witch doctor and helped in a canoe accident.

This has all occurred on the outskirts of dense jungle, not partly explored.

TRIALS

Now Miss Grey has written to her father the Rev.

SPIRITS

Newspaper reports back home

do with a mixture of Malay and sign language. Some of the people seemed bemused that I couldn't understand them when they spoke to me. I don't think they could believe that someone might not speak their language. I suppose that as far as they were concerned it was the only language. I had been teaching myself Malay ever since I set sail from home, and it was disheartening that it wasn't serving me better, though Gwynnedd assured me that most of the men spoke some Malay as well as their tribal tongue and that it would prove useful in the long run.

The men wore ragged shorts or short sarongs tied round their waists. The women were more striking, their only item of clothing being a short black sarong worn from the hips to the knees, while their calves were encircled with brass coils which looked as if they would make walking rather difficult. Both men and women smoked a communal pipe made of bamboo, and when they weren't smoking they chewed a mixture of betel nut, snake skin and tobacco wrapped in a piece of leaf, which stained their lips red. I watched a woman who was cradling a tiny baby transfer the rice that she had been chewing to the mouth of her infant. She smiled when she saw me looking, and I saw that her teeth were blackened stumps.

'I don't think I've ever been the star attraction before,' I said to Gwynnedd, as people continued to come to look at us, showing no embarrassment in doing so.

The only way to put an end to it was to go to bed, though even then we were watched as we undressed. Lying on the straw mats we had been given, covered with a dirty old blanket, I could smell the pigs below, while the sounds of human activity continued from other parts of the longhouse.

'How do you get used to this?' I whispered to Gwynnedd, unsure whether I felt more like laughing or crying.

'Just be thankful there are no rats nibbling our toes,' she replied.

I pulled my knees up towards me with a shudder. I think if I had known some of the sleeping arrangements that awaited me in future weeks, I would have given up and gone home there and then.

I had arrived in Borneo ten days earlier, after a month-long voyage that had started in Tilbury in mid September. The Bishop of Borneo, Nigel Cornwall, whom I had met back in the UK, had been there to meet me on the quay in Kuching, and he and his wife would prove to be most attentive hosts during my time there. I felt a kinship with the place already as I had spent many hours in Newcastle making missal markers to raise funds for its new cathedral, owing to the fact that our own bishop, Noel Hudson, had been a previous bishop in Borneo and retained strong links with his former diocese. I went shopping, I met all sorts of people, I was taken sightseeing and wined and dined. At the club Bishop and Mrs Cornwall attended, I was tickled to see him don a pair of purple swimming trunks with a mitre embroidered on them!

Before I could get too accustomed to this way of life, Gwynnedd Nicholl came to collect me and take me to Padawan, where she ran the clinic, much as I would be doing when I reached my eventual destination of Tongud in British North Borneo, hundreds of miles to the north-east. Gwynnedd, like me, had been sent by the Society for the Propagation of the Gospel (SPG, today USPG – United Society Partners in the Gospel), and she had spent five years in Delhi before arriving in Borneo in 1955. I felt I was in good hands.

And now here I was on a dirty floor in a longhouse, just a few days after dining in the finest hotel in Kuching!

Dawn came, and we were allowed to see our patient. He lay in a filthy state, unable to move. His left leg, twisted and broken below the knee, was very swollen. We washed him gently and gave him morphia. Gwynnedd had chosen two men to help us, and she now explained to them how to reduce the fracture. My role, she told me, was to be the anaesthetist. Gwynnedd was so calm, so sure of my ability as she told me what to do, that as I applied the mask of gauze-covered cotton wool and sprayed it with ethyl chloride, I almost forgot that this was a job for a specially trained doctor and that it would have been unthinkable for me to have been allowed to carry it out back home.

Soon our patient was unconscious. As I continued to monitor him, the men sprang into action, following Gwynnedd's orders. The bones grated as they realigned them, and when Gwynnedd was satisfied with the result she applied plaster of Paris. We elevated his leg on a wooden plank, and our patient regained consciousness.

As Gwynnedd left instructions with his family, I felt pleased and proud to have played my part in the proceedings. However, the thought that I might soon have to perform such operations myself, with no medically trained assistant beside me, was an alarming one.

We ate with the family before setting off for home. I had tried not to think too much about the return journey, assuring myself when I did that it would be easier. In truth, it was worse than the outward one. The rain had made the wooden bridges and logs very slippery, and as the notches on many of the logs were partly worn away, it was often impossible to get a proper grip. The paths were slick with mud, and staying upright was a battle we were constantly losing.

Two or three times we stopped to admire the view of mountain ranges rippling away in the distance, but these moments were all too brief when taking our eyes off the path could mean a potentially fatal fall.

2

'Who will go for us?'

November to December 1959

It was a Sunday afternoon in February 1957 when I broke the news to my parents. We were eating Mum's drop scones round the fire in the vicarage in Stannington, a village near Morpeth in Northumberland that was my father's parish at the time. I remember how delighted they both were to learn that I was thinking of putting myself forward to SPG. It wouldn't be what every parent wanted for their child, and it would mean a long separation, yet they must have known that, in a way, I had been on this path since I was a teenager, my nose stuck in pamphlets about missionaries Mary Slessor in Africa and Gladys Aylward in China. That might sound heavy reading for a girl of that age, but those stories to me were adventures as much as they were tales of faith. They spoke to me about different, exciting lives, about parts of the world I could barely imagine as I grew up in Amble, a town on the North Sea coast, with my younger brother, Joe. In many ways it was a solitary childhood, in which the weekly joy was Girl Guides on a Friday night in the nearby village of Warkworth. As I read the pamphlets, I felt something gnawing away inside me that I realized was an urge to leave home and have adventures myself.

I wanted to be a nurse and, perhaps not surprisingly, left the North-East to train at Charing Cross Hospital in London. I loved my time there, particularly my fourth and final year as the staff nurse on Edward Ward with Sister Pat Phillips, who

Wendy, her parents and her brother Joe, Amble, 1943

was efficient, calm and kind to both staff and patients: qualities I admired and hoped to emulate. We enjoyed our tea breaks in the ward's one and only bathroom, sitting on a wooden board placed over the bath, putting the world to rights.

Sometimes I would catch the No. 9 or No. 27 bus to Kensington to visit my favourite aunt, my mother's sister, Rhoda. Rhoda and I had been close since I was nine years old, when she came to live with us in the vicarage on the outbreak of war. She shocked the folk of Amble by wearing trousers. Well-travelled, fashionable and great fun, she was a joy to spend time with.

I played for the Charing Cross tennis team and was a member of the St Martin Singers at St Martin-in-the-Fields, so I was always busy doing something.

I returned to Newcastle to train as a midwife, and at this life-changing time was enjoying my job as a health visitor in the city, living in a flat in the suburb of Jesmond, close enough to make the most of all the amenities Newcastle had to offer.

One day I attended a talk in the City Hall about missionary work, and was shocked to hear that vast parts of the world had no doctors or nurses to serve them. But it was an article in the *Borneo Chronicle*, which I had subscribed to for some time, that really made my mind up. There I read about two Dayaks from Sarawak – Father Arnold Puntang and catechist Andrew Kiri – who in January 1958 had moved to a remote area to establish the first school in the interior of North Borneo, home to the Dusun ethnic group. Here they were educating 60 children: 56 boys and four girls. They were now looking for either a doctor or a nurse to run a clinic and begin medical work there.

The words they used – which I recognized from Isaiah 6 – touched my heart: 'Whom shall I send? And who will go for us?'

I felt as if Father Puntang and Andrew Kiri were speaking to me personally. I knew that I had to be the one to go.

Once I had made up my mind and had been accepted by SPG, there followed a year at the College of the Ascension in Selly Oak, Birmingham, home at that time to a number of colleges sponsored by different Christian denominations. At times it all seemed to be taking too long and I felt a burning impatience to complete my training and get to Borneo, where I knew I was needed. Yet I enjoyed that year, and it widened my horizons. I learned about Chinese culture and had useful lessons on how to speak in public. In the afternoons I went to the casualty department of the nearest hospital and watched the doctors stitching wounds, though, as a nurse, I wasn't allowed to have a go myself.

Another vivid memory from those days is of attending a Congregational Church service and seeing for the first time a woman administering Holy Communion. It would be many years before I saw it happen again. And yet it seemed and felt absolutely natural.

While I was in Selly Oak, Bishop Cornwall came over on furlough and we talked together about what lay ahead for me. I am sure we must have covered all sorts of subjects, but the one that sticks in my mind is of him telling me, 'Your basic diet will be tapioca.' All I could think of was the tapioca pudding we had eaten during my wartime schooldays. A hot milk pudding sounded a strange thing to be eating in the tropics! I had no idea that tapioca root was the Dusuns' basic food when they had finished their supplies of rice, which was their other staple, nor that, similar to potato, it could be fried to make more porous chips.

The truth was, I had no idea what I was letting myself in for.

And perhaps that was hardly surprising, given the outfit list that arrived from SPG a few weeks before my departure:

1 dressing gown or housecoat
6 slips
6 pairs French knickers to match
4 nightdresses (without sleeves) or pyjamas (nylon, silk or rayon)
4 brassieres and 2 or 3 Aertex girdles
2 or 3 pairs nylon stockings
6 or more cotton day dresses
2 or 3 silk or rayon afternoon dresses
1 short cocktail-party dress
2 or more evening dresses and slips

1 long black evening skirt
1 lightweight woollen cardigan
1 lightweight waterproof
1 or 2 pairs washable summer gloves
1 or 2 small smart straw hats

At the bottom of the list was the advice that a summer vest might be useful in wet weather, along with the warning, 'Hats, shoes and corsetry cannot be obtained. Even though it is hot, I strongly advise every woman to wear an Aertex girdle, *always*. It is a great mistake to let one's figure go, as so many women do.'

I decided that I was going to be better off writing a list of my own.

I set sail from Tilbury on SS *Corfu*. It was like being on holiday. There were cocktails before dinner, wine with it and liqueurs after. I swam in the daytime and danced in the evenings. And I wrote letters to everyone at home, particularly my parents and Rhoda; the congregation at my parish church, St George's, Jesmond; and Miss Elsie Stephenson, who had nursed in the Far East herself and always showed such an interest in my career. I had been working under Miss Stephenson as a district nurse in Newcastle when she called me into her office one day and suggested I train as a health visitor. Not long after, she went to Edinburgh to become director of the first university nursing department in Britain. I had promised to keep in touch.

I teamed up with another single female passenger. Sister Christina of the Companions of Jesus the Good Shepherd (CJGS) was also destined for Borneo, having left her mother house in Devon. She was about my age and was a gentle person of delicate appearance. Sister Christina was going to Sandakan to take charge of a small convent and teach in St Monica's girls' school in the town. Every morning without fail – on deck or in one of our cabins – we sat down together and taught ourselves Malay, ploughing our way through a thick textbook.

In Port Said, where I paddled in the mouth of the Nile, I had my first taste of the East. I had never seen poverty close up like this before, with people pestering me to buy their wares. We sailed, very slowly, through the Suez Canal and I watched the landscape change to desert. As it grew hotter, Sister Christina and I often slept on deck.

In Aden I was struck by the sight of women in purdah, and of an old woman sweeping the streets. Was she as old as she looked, or had the life she led made her look that way? Whichever the answer, it still shocked me.

I realized that I was leaving behind, in the ship's wake, some of my previous assumptions about life. The East would not mean just new sights and experiences but also a change in the way I looked at and thought about things. I was thankful for my strong Christian faith, which I knew would help me to cope.

Our fellow passengers – many of them civil servants or missionaries – were a sociable bunch, and when most of them left the ship in Bombay we were sad to see them go.

There was a state of emergency when we landed in Ceylon. The week before, a Buddhist monk had shot dead the prime minister but, other than soldiers with rifles, there was little sign of disturbance. A few children were begging in the clean, wide streets of Colombo, but they did not look as desperate as some of the beggars we had seen elsewhere.

Three days later we sailed past an island just north of Sumatra, where I had my first glimpse of jungle. I looked at it, awestruck. It seemed both majestic and alien. As we entered the Strait of Malacca and docked on the island of Penang, we ventured into it for the first time, taking a funicular railway to the top of Penang Hill. The sound of crickets and birdsong made us feel a long way from the city below.

Sister Christina and I spent a few days together in Singapore before going our separate ways. Taxis hooted and stopped to offer their services as I set off Christmas shopping down Orchard Road. It was only October, but I wasn't sure if I would have another chance. I also stocked up on reading material in the SPCK (Society for the Promotion of Christian Knowledge) headquarters.

When we parted, as I set sail for Kuching on SS *Perlis*, I felt as if I was saying goodbye to an old friend, but took comfort in the knowledge that we would meet again when I arrived in Sandakan in the new year.

I saw the Borneo coast for the first time on the afternoon of Monday 19 October, a month after setting sail, and the next day was installed in the home of Bishop and Mrs Cornwall in Kuching. As I lay under the ceiling fan in my room, I wondered how a north-eastern lass like myself would ever get used to the heat. Even London summers had sometimes been a challenge!

When Gwynnedd arrived, she took one look at the clothes I had brought before declaring most of them unsuitable and whisking me off shopping for a pair of sturdy canvas boots and some sarongs. She showed me how to fasten a sarong and explained that unless I could be sure of total privacy, I would have to wear one when I was bathing in rivers – the closest I would get to having a proper bath where I was going.

She flashed me a mischievous smile. 'Did you hear what the Dayaks said about you? They told me you were a very nice woman with a beautiful body.'

'Oh,' I said, feeling myself blush a little. 'That's the nicest compliment I've had for a while!'

There was no question of throwing me in at the deep end, for after my spell with Gwynnedd I spent some time with another SPG nurse, Beryl Hobby, in Bunuk, not far from Kuching. Beryl had been there for ten months, and had spent two years in Malaya before attending the College of the Ascension in Selly Oak, as I had done. She was more forthright than patient, gentle Gwynnedd, though just as devoted to her work.

'It's frustrating,' she told me, 'but so many of the ailments you'll see could be eliminated with soap and hot water. Diarrhoea, coughs, running ears, sore eyes and worms. Lots of worms! There's more exciting stuff too – snake bites, appendicitis, that sort of thing.'

I didn't like to say that 'exciting' wasn't the word I would use, though I appreciated that it would be interesting to have a change from run-of-the-mill illnesses.

One morning I accompanied Beryl to the longhouse home of a woman who had been in labour for two days. Despite the heat, an open fire was burning in the room, close to where she lay. On examining her, we found the baby's head in the low cavity and our patient three-quarters dilated. After we had administered pethidine and catheterized her, she made good progress and the baby was delivered two hours later. As I bathed the infant, the old women who had been watching from the corner came forward and began to knead the mother's uterus with great force. They pounded away, using a movement not unlike kneading dough for a loaf of bread.

This fundal pressure failed to expel the placenta, and after examining our patient again we decided to let nature take its course and leave her until the evening.

We returned at 6 p.m. The placenta was still adherent, so Beryl made the decision to induce general anaesthesia with ethyl chloride spray, and informed me that I was to perform the manual removal procedure.

I wondered if I had misheard her. 'But, I don't think . . . '

'If it's your first time, then all the more reason to do it here while I'm with you,' she said briskly.

I had watched a surgeon remove a placenta while I observed at Newcastle General Hospital, but to carry it out myself was another matter. I knew the potential risks, and how delicate the wall of the uterus is. But I could see there was no point in protesting any further.

Tracing the umbilical cord, I was able to reach the placenta, which I found was still attached.

With the mother flat on her back, it was difficult to get my hand round it, and I was soon perspiring heavily. The fire continued to give out a steady heat right beside me. To make matters worse, the room was dark apart from the light we had brought with us – a metal oil lamp with a tiny wick, not much more effective than a candle.

I moved my hand round the placenta with a slicing motion – as I had seen the consultant do. Up and down, from one side to the other. Eventually I felt it become free and fall into my hand. I gently removed it. Beryl examined it, to be sure that it was intact.

She nodded. 'Well done.'

And there was no haemorrhage. I wiped my brow and gave a laugh, which was more of relief than anything else.

Now the old women came forward again and placed the placenta in an earthenware jar lined with leaves. This was filled with ash from the fireplace and left in the room.

Our patient was very drowsy as we prepared to leave, and as her relatives seemed worried about this, we roused her and got her talking to show them all was well. The baby looked healthy, happily sucking at the breasts of the old ladies, one of whom was his grandmother. I suppose they weren't really old at all by Western standards but here, where life expectancy was significantly lower than in the West, they were the senior members of the community and appeared old to my eyes.

We visited our patient again the next morning and were pleased to see that she was well, with no excessive pain and normal blood loss.

I felt I was ready for Tongud after all that had happened so far.

3

A *hut and a jamban*

December 1959 to April 1960

It was Tamu – a big market and social gathering – and all the tribes in the area were converging on Tongud the weekend that Joan and I were due to arrive. Joan Goodricke, an Australian schoolteacher, was going to take charge of the school while I ran the dispensary, giving Father Puntang and Andrew Kiri more time for their mission work. As we would be sharing a house, I was slightly anxious about meeting her as I awaited her return from furlough.

After leaving Beryl I had spent Christmas in Kuching with Bishop Cornwall and his party. It felt strange to be celebrating Christmas in the heat, and to see carol singers wearing summer dresses and sandals! As we sat down to our turkey, I thought of my parents doing the same back home at exactly the same time – 12.30 p.m. for them, 8.30 p.m. for us.

I met a British man called Lawrence Jones who was in charge of the Sarawak and North Borneo census. At five foot ten, he was a couple of inches taller than me, slimly built and dark haired. He took me under his wing, driving me around the countryside, and invited the Cornwalls and me to his home for a meal one evening. One day I went to hear him talk about the population figures. I think that was when it truly struck me how isolated my new home would be. I learned that I would be living in the largest and least populated district of the colony and that, according to the 1951 census, there were a mere 1.5 people per square mile.

Wendy's friend, the census chief Lawrence Jones

'No shops, no restaurants,' said Lawrence, as he drove me back to the bishop's. 'No friend round the corner! How do you think you'll find it?'

I replied that it would be a challenge, but one that I was ready to face.

In mid January I left Kuching and sailed up the coast to Jesselton, capital of North Borneo. The views from the boat reminded me of Scotland, and gave me my first glimpse of Mount Kinabalu, the highest peak on the island. From there I sailed to Sandakan to be reunited with Sister Christina and prepare for Tongud.

Sandakan was a mixture of multi-storey and more traditional buildings, with a busy port. I stayed in the boarding house in the grounds of St Monica's School with two teachers. Barbara Beaumont was a fellow Brit whom I had met in Selly Oak, while Jean Durrant came from Australia.

The Anglican buildings were on a compound together on Elton Hill, named after William Elton, the first SPG missionary in North Borneo, and founder of the secondary school, St Michael's, whose pupils had been taught in a building dubbed the Cattle Shed in the immediate aftermath of the war. An attractive two-storey building stood in its place now. It was a downhill walk into town – to the shops and the post office – along roads whose lush greenness reminded me of the British countryside, though the large-leaved plants and the insects attracted to them would have been alien to people at home, as would the tropical heat. On my way I passed the tennis court and the cinema, and at the bottom, on the other side of the main road, lay the sea. Sometimes I saw women labourers, who wore veils over their wide-brimmed hats to protect their faces from the sun.

In my room, escaping from the heat and thick humidity, I could hear through the open windows Sister Christina and school principal, Sister Florence, teaching English to the girls, the young voices chanting, 'That is good. That is better. And that is the best of all!'

Not that I had much time for sitting round. I discovered that no preparations had been made for equipping the dispensary and so I had to start to gather equipment and medicines, many of them donated from Australia and the UK as well as the local Red Cross. There was personal shopping to do and provisions to buy, as there were no shops where I was going. I sent several boxes ahead, including my record player and a package that had arrived from SPG for which I had to pay a small fortune at customs. I hoped it would prove to be worth the expense when I had time to unpack it.

I also spent a lot of time in the outpatients department of the hospital and the dental clinic. Sometimes, as I watched the dentists extracting teeth and the doctors dealing with injuries and illnesses that ranged from the trivial to the serious, I felt a knot of anxiety tightening inside me, as I wondered what I might have to deal with on my own, with no one close at hand to ask for advice. When we had time, Sister Christina and I carried on with our Malay lessons, while I also tried to learn some words of Dusun. In the evenings, Jean, Barbara, the sisters and I talked and played Scrabble. Those were happy and comfortable hours.

In Sandakan I met a man who would become one of the most important people in my life in Borneo; he had, indeed, been responsible for my being here in the first place. Frank Lomax, a British Anglican priest, had sailed to Borneo with his wife, Irene, in 1950 and been sent to Sandakan by Bishop Cornwall. The bishop had presented the couple with a copy of *Hakka-Chinese Lessons*, Hakka being the predominant tongue of the Chinese immigrants who had been brought to work in the town by the British. Frank would prove to be an accomplished linguist.

'Ah! Another Geordie!' said the man in baggy shorts, as we met outside St Michael's Church, one of the few stone-built buildings in North Borneo.

He was at least six feet tall, slim and strong. I don't know if to this day I have ever met anyone as active as Frank, for he seemed to be always on the go. I never knew him to take a siesta, which was considered normal – sensible, even – in the tropics.

'Are you one too?' I asked him.

'As good as. I went to school in Lancashire, but I was ordained by Noel Hudson and served my title in Byker, which is where Irene is from. Her father had a butcher's shop there. We both think of the North-East as home.'

I thought of Byker in the East End of Newcastle, with its breezy brick terraces running down to the River Tyne – once-mighty river of shipbuilding and industry. And I looked at St Michael's, pretty enough to grace a home counties village, its well-cared-for lawns fringed with colourful tropical plants.

'Coming here must have been quite a change, Father Lomax.'

'Frank, please! Now come and meet the family.'

Irene was as friendly and down-to-earth as her husband, and the couple had an eight-year-old son, Michael. Over a cup of tea and a slice of Irene's lemon cake in the rectory, Frank told me about their arrival in Borneo from Newcastle.

'We've watched Sandakan get back on its feet after the war. You should have seen it then, Wendy.' He shook his head at the memory. 'It had been devastated by bombing as the British tried to get rid of the Japanese invaders. And you'll have heard of the Sandakan Death Marches . . . The church was one of the few buildings to survive. Even the banks were made of *kajang* [woven palm leaves] and *atap* [palm-leaf roofing]. It had been the capital of North Borneo before that, but the new government moved the capital to Jesselton, though that was a mess too.'

But Frank always knew that his main mission lay with the people in the interior, and a few years later he travelled with a government surveyor called Bruce Sandilands, first up the Labuk and then up the Kinabatangan, a 350-mile-long river that has its outlet in the Sulu Sea, close to Sandakan. Bruce Sandilands, a committed Christian who worshipped in Frank's church, had first arrived in Borneo in 1949 and had got to know this wild area well. He had seen the desperate living conditions of many of the people: the disease and high infant mortality rate, the lack of schools and medical care, the poor agricultural methods. Meeting with the local *orang tuas* or OTs (headmen), Frank and Bruce found them open to the suggestion of having mission schools and clinics in their kampongs, and from that trip the North Borneo Interior Mission (NBIM) was born. Tongud, where they established the Mission of the Epiphany, was the very first.

Despite little external money for these plans – the first funding came from a Lent-box collection in his parish of St Michael's – Frank was a man who made things happen.

In the long talks I had with Frank before setting out, my feeling that I was doing the right thing was strengthened, though I had to admit to some trepidation.

The day Joan returned from furlough we sat on my bed and talked non-stop into the night. Joan was an attractive young woman of 26, four years younger than me. She was almost as tall as me, slim, with short, dark, wavy hair, and she had a gentle smile. She had been teaching in St Monica's School for three years when she had decided she would like to go into the interior.

'But Frank wasn't keen to let me go on my own. Oh Wendy, I thanked God when I heard you had volunteered and they told me we could go together!'

I can truly say that we clicked straightaway. We had a lot in common. We were both the daughters of vicars, for a start, but I also discovered something else.

'I was born in Berkshire, but Dad was curate at St Gabriel's in Heaton [a suburb of Newcastle] for a while before we moved back down south.'

The world suddenly seemed a much smaller place. I laughed delightedly. 'First I discover that Frank and Irene are Geordies, and now you!'

Joan said that her father had been a successful accountant before becoming a priest, and later took the family to settle in Tasmania. Joan was 16 years old when they sailed.

Like myself, I suppose, this teacher was driven to serve others by her strong faith. She seemed quiet and self-contained, but I could sense a core of steel, a quality I would see more of in the months ahead.

Irene and Michael Lomax, Sisters Christina and Florence, and Barbara and Jean waved us off on the quay as we set sail for Tongud at 7 p.m. in the evening of Sunday 24 April 1960. I felt a pang as I watched my new friends getting smaller and smaller.

It being Tamu, there were several of us in the *Mantanani*, a government launch. As well as Frank, Joan, our boatmen and myself, there was the Resident, Keith Wookey, a senior government official and a man with a reputation for having a strong affinity with the people of Borneo; Bishop Wong, Assistant Bishop of Borneo; Dr Christiansen from the hospital in Sandakan; and Martin Wilson, a young British man serving with the organization Voluntary Service Overseas. Tamu, I would discover, was a big draw, both an administrative and a commercial opportunity – with the tribal chiefs and many of their people together in the same place – but also a chance for everyone to let their hair down.

As we set off, I could not begin to know how many times over the next two and a half years I would make the voyage that lay ahead.

The first part of the journey was a sea crossing, which I had been told could be rough, but our powerful launch negotiated it with ease and we moored at the mouth of the

River Kinabatangan overnight. Joan and I slept on the open deck on lilos, beside the bridge. It was surprisingly cool and windy.

We set off again at 5 a.m. and travelled all day. This part of the river, near its mouth, was wide and muddy.

Joan and I cooked lunch for the party, but as we managed to burn the rice and produce an unbearably hot fish curry, the men decided to take charge of the evening meal.

We passed a timber camp, with huge logs piled up close to the shore, and an abandoned settlement where a dilapidated school building looked as if it was being consumed by the forest. As we neared Lamag, I saw monkeys taking huge leaps from tree to tree.

Lamag, the administrative centre for the Kinabatangan area, had a small, poorly equipped dispensary, a shop and a government office, where the next morning I posted a couple of letters – and found one waiting for me. To my surprise it was from Lawrence. After we had got to know each other in Kuching, Lawrence had turned up while I was in Sandakan, where he liked to take me on his favourite walk, up a hill to a Chinese cemetery. There we sat to admire the view of the town – the buildings with their red, blue and green rooftops, backed by the blue bay and the Sulu Sea. He reminded me of this in his letter and told me how much he had enjoyed my company, before wishing me well in my posting.

Joan saw me smiling. 'From someone special?'

'Oh, Lawrence is charming. It's just a surprise to hear from him so soon!'

The River Kinabatangan changes from one stretch to the next – from deep to shallow, from sluggish to rapid, from wide to so narrow the trees on each bank brush the sides of the vessel as you pass. Because of this, the journey from Sandakan to Tongud cannot usually be undertaken in one boat, but suitable ones are picked up from posts along the way, where supplies of petrol can also be borrowed or bought. And so that morning we unloaded everything from the *Mantanani* and transferred it all to two smaller boats.

Joan, Frank, Bishop Wong and I set off from Lamag on the *Malaikat* (which means 'angel' or 'messenger' in Malay), a launch with an enclosed cabin belonging to the Tongud mission.

'The trick is never to be in a hurry,' said Frank, as we watched the rest of our party zoom off in a sleek motorboat. 'Besides, you see more at this speed.'

For many miles of our journey there was actually little to see except the brown water and the thick green vegetation on the shore that hid everything within it. Sometimes a splash or a ripple would hint at some fish or river creature, or a kingfisher would flit across our path before disappearing into the trees. But there was always plenty to hear – screeches coming from the forest, strange cries and hootings.

Frank, Bishop Wong and Joan on their way to Tongud

I remembered the figures that Lawrence had shown me about the population of this part of North Borneo. Here was the proof of them! I felt as if I was journeying into the middle of nowhere. Thinking of shabby, bustling Sandakan, where the school bells had punctuated my days, I felt a pang of homesickness for my home of the past weeks among the nuns and teachers.

The next night, in a timber camp, the workers gave us hot water to wash in, which was very welcome – and the beer even more so. We were shown to the guest room, so small that the four camp beds inside it were almost touching each other. In truth it was hardly any different from our sleeping arrangements on the boat, but something about the neat beds made it seem more intimate. However, a bed was a bed, and Bishop Wong and Frank posed no threat to our virtue! I expected to fall asleep quickly, but a group of Chinese workers playing a noisy game of mahjong in the room next door kept me awake.

We arrived at a timber estate at lunchtime the following day to find it was the birthday of the manager, Ray Kelly. He made a fuss of us all and served us ham, new potatoes and salad. Our welcome the night after in Tangkulap, the last stop before our destination, was less friendly. There, the next morning, it was time to change boats again, and we unloaded everything from *Malaikat* and fitted as much as we could into *Bintang* (meaning 'star') *Epiphany*, a canoe with an outboard motor belonging to the mission, as the water was too low for *Malaikat* to travel further upriver.

We reached Tongud at 4 p.m. on our fifth day of sailing. It seemed to come out of nowhere. The first indication that we were getting close was the sound of chatter, which quickly turned into cheering. The jetty was lined with people, the most numerous being children. There, too, were our earlier travelling companions – Mr Wookey, Dr Christiansen and Martin Wilson – all waving and looking pleased to see us.

As we disembarked – if that is not too grand a word for stepping out of such a basic vessel – a smiling man came towards us and introduced himself as Father Arnold Puntang. Here was the man whose words had propelled me from my comfortable life in Newcastle to the other side of the world! He was a few inches shorter than me (though at five foot eight I was getting used to being taller than most of the people I met in Borneo), slight and of youthful appearance. But even on that first meeting I sensed his wisdom and calm authority. Fellow founder of the mission, Andrew Kiri, about my height and gangly, shook my hand with the same easy smile as Father Puntang.

Tongud had a buzz about it that afternoon – a feeling of preparation, of impending festivities – as people arrived for Tamu and greeted old friends.

Father Puntang led the way from the jetty. He pointed to the left, where the main buildings of the kampong were situated close to the river. We carried on uphill along a mud track cut through the long grass to the site of the mission, seeing some of the temporary camps set up by the visitors for Tamu on the way. Schoolboys helped to carry our belongings, looking at us with unabashed interest as they scampered along at our side.

We passed a group of men who looked the worse for drink.

'It isn't usually like this,' said Father Puntang apologetically. 'But some of these people have travelled a long way to be here, and it's a special occasion.'

I must confess that when he showed us the house that was to be our home for the next two and a half years, my heart sank. It was raised on wooden posts three feet from the ground – 'to keep out snakes and scorpions', he said – and had a palm-leaf roof. We climbed the steps and Father Puntang opened the door to a rather gloomy interior. The walls – which had large gaps in them – were made of bark and the floor of slatted bamboo, like the floors in the longhouse. Father Puntang admitted that the walls did not look very attractive and said he would arrange to have them covered with sheets of newspaper, which he had done in the house he and Andrew shared. Guessing that Joan's expression echoed my own thoughts, I quickly said I thought we would prefer them left as they were.

'Of course Andrew can make you whatever else you need,' he added, trying to open a window that refused to budge. 'He is a very skilled carpenter, you know.'

There was a living room, two bedrooms and a kitchen. The living room contained a table, an oil lamp and two chairs.

The house made of bamboo, bark and palm leaves that
Wendy and Joan shared

The tiny bedrooms were separated by a curtain, and each contained a bed and a small chest of drawers. Sure enough, all the furniture had been made by Andrew. The kitchen had a bench, a Primus stove and an oven, 12 inches square. A large drum that had once held petrol sat on a platform at the side of the house and collected rainwater from a bamboo channel that ran along the roof. This was our drinking water as well as water for washing.

I was glad that while I'd been in Sandakan I'd spent some time choosing material I could turn into curtains, as well as purchasing a few knick-knacks that would make it feel more homely, as this place really was rather spartan. A hut was probably a better description than a house.

'And there is your *jamban*,' said Father Puntang, pointing to a cluster of trees about 30 yards away. I could just make out the palm-leaf roof of our lavatory. 'But watch your step as you go – snakes and scorpions like the long grass.'

As we headed off to see the other mission buildings, he added, 'Please call me Arnold.'

Frank and Bishop Wong were to be housed with Joan and me, and the rest of the visitors were sleeping in the dispensary – an old wooden building in need of some repair, but more substantial than others I had seen. Eight steps led up to a small entrance and waiting area, housing a bench. Inside was a reasonably sized consulting room with two small wards leading off it, where inpatients could stay, a kitchen and a store room.

'Andrew built the beds,' said Arnold, as he showed us round. 'We've been using one of the wards as a chapel but we'll use a room in the school from now on. We've begun to build our own church, but it's not finished yet.'

In fact the church, whose foundations we saw on our tour, had barely been started. The rest of the mission consisted of a house shared by Arnold and Andrew, the school and the boys' boarding house. In spite of Lawrence's warning, the kampong of Tongud did have a store, along with about 40 homes, many of them without walls and far more basic-looking than ours.

After our tour, Joan and I did some unpacking.

'What do you think?' I asked her, as I trod rather dubiously on a bamboo slat. I added, 'I think I might be too big for this house!'

'I think flimsy is the word I would use,' she replied.

'My thoughts entirely.'

It was difficult to concentrate with so much going on. We gave up and joined the guests in the dispensary, and helped Arnold, who was cooking for us all.

I got chatting to Martin Wilson, who told me he had been teaching for six months and was about to take up a posting with the census office in Lamag, after seeing what Tamu was all about. I learned that Martin was the son of Leonard Wilson, the Bishop of Birmingham, who had grown up in Low Fell and was a childhood friend of my father. Once again, home suddenly felt a lot closer. Leonard Wilson had been the Bishop of Singapore when the Second World War broke out, and had been interned and tortured by the Japanese.

Later, Frank and Bishop Wong slept in Joan's room and she shared mine. The sound of all the revelry kept me awake as I lay in my new home that first night – that and a thousand thoughts that were jostling in my mind.

The next day, the start of Tamu, Arnold and Frank – Frank wearing a white alb over his shorts – baptized 50 people of all ages in the river. This was followed by the confirmation of a similar number by Bishop Wong.

'I'm so glad you're here to see this, Wendy,' Frank told me, his eyes shining. 'It's a wonderful way to mark the start of your service. When I think how the government told us it wasn't worth our trouble coming here – too far away, too hard to get to, too sparsely populated! Today is the culmination of Bruce's vision all those years ago.'

In addition to the purposes served by Tamu – political, social, commercial – it afforded those living in even more isolated places than Tongud the opportunity to see a doctor or a nurse. I therefore spent the day with Dr Christiansen attending to a long stream of patients. Beryl had been right – most of them presented problems that were easy to treat.

Baptism at Tongud, with Arnold Puntang, Frank Lomax and the boatman, Majang, holding candles in a bag

I cleaned and dressed wounds, I drained boils, I applied balm to sores. Much of what I was treating could have been avoided in the first place with basic hygiene. Having seen people wash, defecate in and drink from the same stretch of river, I realized that health education was going to be an important part of my job – and perhaps not an easy one.

I also saw my first yaws patient. Yaws is a tropical disease which affects the skin, bone and cartilage. A bacterium causes a skin lesion which, if left untreated, leads to further lesions and, over time, to chronic disfigurement. The man standing before me, who gave a wide toothless grin, had no nose, just a huge, pus-filled cavity. His forehead and the area around his eyes were covered in bumps and crusted sores, and a sore partly covered one eye. It pained me to see another human being looking like this, and upset me even more to see him so cheerful, so grateful for our attention. We could treat him with antibiotics, but it was too late to save his nose. When Dr Christiansen told me that yaws primarily affected children and that it was easily passed on among those living in close proximity in longhouses or other insanitary dwellings, I resolved to make this a personal project and to find out as much as I could about this cruel disease.

The following day the dispensary became a marketplace as people brought their wares to buy, sell and barter. There were things made from bamboo, wood and palm leaves. Ingenious rat traps and fish traps. Live animals in crates and cages, and dead ones slung unceremoniously on top of each other. I saw the *durian*, a large thorny fruit with a strong odour. Gwynnedd had given me one, and had laughed when she saw how I was almost ill at the taste of it. I couldn't believe that she actually liked it, and she admitted that it wasn't most Westerners' cup of tea. There were things that might have been edible or might have served some other purpose – they were alien to my eyes and I had no way of telling. There were blowpipes, swords and knives; musical instruments and beadwork jewellery.

Dr Christiansen said he wanted to buy me something and asked what I would like. I felt awkward choosing a gift, but when he picked up a mat woven from rattan I realized that it was just what we needed in our new home to prevent small items from falling through the floor to the ground below, and I happily accepted it. I tried not to look too shocked when he bought himself a live salamander, a tortoise and a honey bear (also known as a sun bear, the smallest of the bear family and indigenous to south-east Asia). OT Harun, the headman in Tongud – a Muslim, like the other OTs in the region – presented me with a parang, the handle of which was beautifully carved. I thanked him profusely, thinking, with a chuckle, that it made a change from soap or a box of handkerchiefs.

That night Tamu turned into a giant party. After we had eaten, Joan and I went to see what was happening. The locals were dancing a slow, mournful dance and drinking *tapai*, an alcoholic beverage made from fermented tapioca root which they drank from a large earthenware jar through a communal bamboo straw. They offered us a glass of it and I took just a few sips to be polite, knowing its base was unboiled river water. We joined in the dancing for a while before heading for our beds.

It felt awful to wave goodbye to Frank, Bishop Wong and the others the next morning after breakfast, but at last I had some time to do more unpacking and take in my new surroundings, as well as relax. The music had gone on for much of the previous night and I didn't feel very rested.

The following day I woke up with a ghastly stomach cramp and nausea. Stumbling back to the house from the jamban I felt weak and dizzy. It was only 6.30 a.m., but the heat was already taking hold of the thick air. I went back to bed but soon needed the loo again. The pain temporarily relieved, I saw a line of patients already forming outside the door of the dispensary. I had no option but to put on my uniform – one of four simple white dresses I had had made by a Chinese tailor in Sandakan – and go to attend them.

My first day in charge passed in a blur. I suppose you might call it an organized muddle, punctuated with frequent rushes to the jamban, washing my hands so thoroughly after each visit that they were soon almost as tender as my poor stomach. I managed to make myself understood with a mixture of my basic Malay and sign language. Somewhere in my boxes lay something that would have proved very useful – an anatomy flannelgraph. Flannelgraphs are flannel boards with cut-out items or people, used usually to tell stories, and helpful in both my medical and missionary work. However, there was no time to go hunting for this one, and most of the boxes remained unpacked.

By the time evening came I was in a state of collapse, still vomiting and with attacks of dysentery.

I wasn't much better the next morning, but Andrew came to help interpret in the dispensary, which made things easier. In the afternoon I finally made a start on unpacking the medicines and getting the place how I wanted it.

Stumbling into my bedroom that evening, I was confronted by the sight of a giant scorpion on the wall. It was both grotesque and fascinating at the same time. With its exaggerated claws and long lethal tail, it was almost a parody of itself. I had been warned about looking out for scorpions on the ground, and told how they liked to hide under wood or in crevices, so what was it doing displaying itself so blatantly in my bedroom?

My first thought was to go and find help, but I knew the others were busy, and besides, I wasn't going to be able to do that every time I was frightened by something. Should I ignore it, and hope that it would leave of its own accord? No, even safely ensconced in my mosquito net I wouldn't be able to relax, knowing it was there. I looked round the room, without much hope, and there it was – the parang I had been given by the OT! Without giving the process too much thought – which was probably very unwise of me – I got as close as I dared to the creature and stabbed it. Its body twisted and thrashed for a few seconds before it went still.

Then I flung myself on to my bed, not sure whether to laugh or cry.

Joan returned a short while later, by which time I had calmed down and was lying reading, and disposed of it for me.

'You might be the nurse, but you haven't eaten for days,' she said, putting a plate and a hot drink in front of me. 'You're just going to get weaker. See if you can force something down.'

Remembering how my father used to bring me hot milk with brandy and sugar when I was ill in bed with a cold, I felt my eyes sting.

'Joan, I'm glad you're here. I feel so useless,' I confessed.

'Don't be silly. Everyone gets sick in Borneo, you mark my words. But you need to listen to your body and rest more.'

I nibbled the dry cracker, reluctantly at first, then I realized how hungry I was and wolfed the rest of it down.

I felt slightly stronger the next day and carried on with my unpacking and sorting. I began to make out record cards for the patients. Later I went to the river to bathe and wash some clothes. I woke the following morning with a sore throat, runny nose and headache.

I began to wonder if I would ever feel well again.

4

The operating theatre

May 1960

As I was going to bed one night I heard loud wailing coming from the kampong. My cold was drying up and I had been hoping for an uninterrupted night's sleep, which was now beginning to look unlikely. I made a mental note to ask Mum to send me some ear plugs in her next parcel.

The wailing had stopped by morning but started up again around lunchtime. Arnold said it was a *mameow,* or medical witchcraft, being practised on the wife of Ongkila, whom I had been treating for malaria. He accompanied Joan and me down to the kampong as I took more medicine. Joan had her camera with her.

Outside Ongkila's house was a palm-leaf shelter, under which sat the wailing women. One of them was Dalila, Tongud's medicine woman. There were lots of other people around, drinking tapai and cooking and eating. Beside the women was a basket containing a live pig, and next to that two bowls.

Arnold said that the traditional belief of the people was that sickness was caused by an evil spirit entering the sufferer. The purpose of the pig was to tempt the spirit to leave the patient – pigs being the most popular victims of evil spirits – to allow the person's lost soul to return. At some point they would kill the pig, and certain rituals would be performed with its blood. I was astonished to recognize some of the people present as self-professed Christians who

Wendy visits a patient receiving traditional medicine from local women, who sit under a palm-leaf shelter

attended our services. I suppose that was the moment when I became aware of some of the challenges that faced us.

I learned that Arnold believed that it was not his place to condemn or put a stop to these practices, but to gain acceptance through trust and example. You might say he won people over through his love for them all.

Later, talking to Joan, I commented that my patient had received both ancient and modern medicine that day. But a thought struck me.

'Will they attribute her recovery to the pig – or to my penicillin and Nivaquine?'

Life was slowly beginning to settle into a comfortable pattern – or perhaps 'comfortable' is not the right word to use in a place of constant heat and humidity, with the temperature in the high eighties (over 30 degrees Celsius) every day.

Joan and I lived in close proximity in our simple home, a curtain dividing our bedrooms. If one of us started over an insect, moaned in our sleep or sighed as we prepared to get out of bed to begin the day ahead, the other heard it. Having grown up in large vicarages, where I had had my own bedroom (though I had occasionally shared a room during my years of nursing), it was the closest I had lived to another person, and today it strikes me more than ever how fortunate it was that we got on from the start. We were both very busy in our work, but we always sat down to eat together, taking it in turns to cook. There was always plenty to talk about, for a day in the dispensary was as varied as one in the school.

'Do you know how the children count?' she asked me one day. 'They use the three joints on each finger, so they can count up to 15 on one hand.'

I thought this was ingenious. As the pupils went barefoot, I asked if they used their toes as well, but Joan said that she drew the line at feet on desks.

'Anyway, I'm hoping to get them all kitted out in plimsolls when I have some spare funds. Sometimes it's hard to decide how to prioritize – footwear and more substantial clothes, or reading materials? I suppose I can make my own books for them, but I'm not really a cobbler.'

She was, though, a very skilled seamstress. I could sew well enough – curtains, cushion covers and such – but if something needed a more expert hand, I was thankful to have Joan to turn to. We also both liked to be quiet, and appreciated being left alone to read, write or think.

Arnold led us in daily worship: Mass at 6.30 a.m. four times a week, Matins the other three days and Evensong every day –

on Sundays in Dusun, Malay and English. School hours for the pupils (of whom the average age was 12) were from 8.30 a.m. to 12.30 p.m., during which they followed the same syllabus as town schools. Before school they worked on the land with Arnold and Andrew, learning how to prepare terraces for rubber trees, and planting fruit and vegetables. Between 3 and 4 p.m. they carried out building and repair work, and between 7 and 9 p.m. they had homework to do. Some of the older teenage boys lent a hand with the younger ones as well as learning engineering skills, including maintenance of the mission's boats. Over time, thanks to these extracurricular activities, Joan and I would gain a small extension on the end of our kitchen and a desk and cupboard each for our bedrooms. Now that Joan had taken charge of the school, Arnold had more time to devote to overseeing these practical tasks, as well as to translating services, hymns and prayers into Dusun – of which there were several related languages and even more dialects.

Three mornings a week, at 7.30 a.m., we spoke via radio to Frank in Sandakan. It was comforting to hear him, to picture him and Irene in the rectory, a wise and warm link with the outside world. But it served a more serious purpose, too – the chance to receive and send messages that otherwise might take days to arrive. Unfortunately, reception was a hit and miss affair and there were times when interference made it difficult to hear each other, or where contact failed altogether. But today I was anxious to speak to him to discuss a patient who had arrived the day before.

Ulor had turned up at the dispensary on his father's back. They had made their way by boat and on foot from their kampong up the River Tongud. A young man in his mid twenties, with a wife and child who also accompanied him, Ulor had acute arthritis in his left knee and a high fever. I suspected an advanced state of septicaemia. The knee was the size of a football and walking had become impossible.

Wendy calls Sandakan via the radio in Arnold's house

His condition was deteriorating. As I stitched the scalp of a boy who had split it open with a parang, and kept an eye on a pneumonia patient in one of the wards, I wondered what I was going to do.

Via the radio I was able to ask Frank to seek advice from Dr Christiansen. I didn't like the idea of performing surgery on a knee, and while I dreaded the thought of the five-day journey to hospital in Sandakan so soon after my arrival, I felt it was preferable to operating myself.

We radioed again the next morning for the answer, and Dr Christiansen's reply was very clear: I was to operate on Ulor without delay.

I spent ages with my copy of *Gray's Anatomy*, identifying the blood vessels and nerves closest to the knee. I couldn't help feeling that this was an area best left to the specialists, but I knew my intervention could save my patient's life.

'I'll need all of you to help me,' I told Arnold, Andrew and Joan.

The men looked uncertain, but they agreed to do what I asked them. Before the operation, the four of us prayed together.

The pneumonia patient had recovered and gone home as I turned the dispensary into an operating theatre. (We always called it the dispensary, but in truth, 'clinic' or even 'hospital' would have been more apt!) The instruments had all been boiled on the Primus stove and everything was to hand. With Ulor on my makeshift operating table I applied the metal mask, which was covered with lint and on to which I sprayed ethyl chloride. Soon he was asleep. Joan was in charge of keeping the mask in place, while Arnold and Andrew were to hand me the instruments when I needed them. As soon as I made the first incision, pus began to flow out of the knee. One bowl, then another. I had never seen so much of it come from one place.

I was concentrating intently, and when I next looked up Arnold and Andrew were disappearing out through the doorway. So much for my assistants! Joan raised her eyes at me over her mask. Thank goodness one of my helpers had a strong stomach.

When I was satisfied that the area was clean, I inserted a drainage tube and closed the wound with catgut and five nylon sutures. Ulor came round and I put him to bed in one of the small wards.

At 4.30 p.m. I radioed Frank to report that all had gone well, and arranged to call again the next morning to talk to Dr Christiansen.

Ulor seemed much better when I went to see him first thing the next morning; his temperature had come down to 97.2 degrees. This was a relief, as Arnold was talking about the two of us setting off on an expedition to a place called

Telupid, where Frank wanted us to pursue the possibility of a mission school. I had made it clear I would not leave my patient until I was sure he was on the mend.

I renewed the dressing and shortened the drainage tube. Dr Christiansen sounded happy when I gave him my report.

As I began to plan for the trip, Ongkila, the husband of the malaria patient, brought Joan and me some fish he had caught – the first I had eaten in Tongud – to say thank you for helping his wife. Remembering how with Gwynnedd we had not been allowed to see our patient until the witch doctor had finished his ministrations, I thought with some satisfaction that local witchcraft and Western medicine were coming together more successfully here. We asked Ongkila if he might be able to supply us with fish twice a week. It would be a welcome addition to our diet.

Joan and I shared cooking duties, doing a week at a time. Most of our food in Tongud came by boat from Sandakan for there was – as yet – little fresh food grown. The locals ate a restricted diet based around rice and tapioca root. We kept our own as varied as possible with canned meat, vegetables and fruit from the town, and fresh meat when Arnold went hunting. We'd been given a scrawny hen by the *Panglima*, a tribal chief and a person of some distinction in the kampong; it lived under the house, and we hoped that it might provide us with a meal one day when it was fatter. We made our own bread, leaving it to rise on one of the steps before baking it in our tiny oven. The flour was full of weevils but there was nothing we could do about that. And, like the locals, we ate a lot of rice and tapioca, slicing the root and turning it into tapioca chips. They needed spice to give them any flavour and had little nutritional value, but at least they were filling.

The next day Ulor's temperature had risen, and it continued to rise all day. I told Arnold we might have to postpone our trip.

'I hope he's going to be OK,' I said to Joan that evening.

We were going down to the river to wash. Arnold had supervised the pupils in cutting a rough path to a section of the River Tongud, just beyond where it divided from the Kinabatangan, and only a short walk from our hut. He said it would make an excellent bathing spot for us both, away from prying eyes.

'He was doing so well,' I continued. 'At times, our Western medicines have such an immediate impact, they shock me as much as the patient.'

'Such as?' asked Joan, as we left our sarongs on the bank and slipped into the water.

'When I was staying with Gwynnedd we were summoned one day to a woman who was supposed to be dying. I think Gwynnedd must have been sceptical from the start, because she sent me in her place. After a two-hour walk I arrived in the village and found the woman lying in agony in her room, surrounded by interested spectators. She wouldn't let anyone near her, apart from me, and when I examined her I saw that she had genital herpes. I applied calamine lotion and gave her pethidine for the pain and Phenergan as an antihistamine. A few minutes later she informed the crowd that the pain was gone, stood up and shooed them all away. I felt like a miracle-worker for a second!'

Joan laughed. 'Then make it stop raining, please!'

The rain, which had started on our walk, was getting heavier. All the same, it felt liberating to be naked in the water, to wash away the sweat and dirt, to cool down, however temporarily. A sudden flash of lightning lit us up like actors on a stage.

'I hope this really is private,' said Joan, looking over her shoulder.

'Does it bother you, being stared at all the time? It cheeses me off sometimes.'

Joan thought before replying. 'I've had longer to get used to it, though it wasn't as blatant in Sandakan. The townsfolk are used to Westerners. But I suppose when you've been brought up being told that modesty is one of woman's greatest virtues, it takes a while.'

After we had finished bathing it was very dark and we couldn't find our sarongs and torches, which we had left on the bank. We scrambled around in the mud, searching for them, laughing so hard I'm surprised no one heard us and came to see what was happening. By the time we got back to the house we were sweating again, and dirtier than when we had set out.

If I had ever felt like a miracle-worker, I realized my limits when, the next day, a man came to the dispensary asking for medicine to make his wife have a son. I had to admit that I was unable to help him. But at least Ulor's temperature had gone down again, and I removed three of the sutures. I told Arnold we could begin to get ready for Telupid.

5

Travels with Arnold

May to June 1960

Arnold and I would make many trips together during the course of my stay – too many for me to include them all in this book. While the trip to Telupid had an additional purpose, they all tended to follow a similar pattern. We would spend the hours of daylight travelling to the kampong, whether on foot, water or – most often – both. On our arrival, someone would bang a gong to announce my clinic. I would see patients until it got dark, after which Arnold and I would eat with the men. Then Arnold would preach and everyone – men, women and children – would sit and listen. I assisted him by using a flannelgraph to tell Bible stories, which fascinated them. When he had finished, a row of gongs of all different sizes would start up, along with other music, and everyone would take a turn to drink tapai out of a big jar. We would be expected to drink too, and I would either take a small sip or pretend to.

Then began the big entertainment for the people: seeing us – particularly me – get ready for bed! We would lie down, perhaps in a room of our own, but more often with the rest of the people and the dogs. Longhouses were less common among the Dusuns than they were among the Dayaks of Sarawak, so we might be in a very basic dwelling with no walls, or in the larger home of the OT. Often the partying would disturb my sleep, and I would rise at daylight feeling unrested. I would see more patients, we would eat rice and then we would set off to the next kampong, the whole routine beginning again.

Telupid lies on the River Labuk, about 30 miles north of Tongud as the crow flies. An overgrown track reputedly linked the two places, but no one knew the way, and it would have been too dangerous to attempt it without knowledgeable guides. Our journey would therefore be a complicated one involving travelling on various rivers as well as long stretches on foot through the jungle.

In the late afternoon on the first day we reached a place called Karamuak, where I held a clinic until it was dark. Arnold and I slept in the same room in a small Chinese store. I saw more patients the next morning before we set off up the River Karamuak in our *perhau*, a tiny dugout canoe, with two men paddling. Progress was very slow. We stopped to eat in a kampong with only three or four houses, and as Arnold cooked our rice I attended to patients. A teenage girl screamed and ran away when she first saw me. Arnold said that she had never seen a white woman before.

At about 5 p.m. we reached a pebbly bank where we set up camp for the night. Arnold made a fire and began to cook as I put up a small tent. Darkness came quickly and there was nothing to do when we had eaten but go to bed and prepare for an early start. I had been grateful for the tent space of my own, but it was so hot inside that I came out and ended up lying down beside the three men.

The forest makes noises at night that it does not make during the day, and the enveloping darkness heightens the senses. I was aware of snapping twigs and the swishing of plants as nocturnal creatures made their stealthy journeys not far from where we lay. The sound of insects was as constant and rhythmical as a machine. I must have slept because a sound broke into my dream that turned out to be rain falling nearby. Arnold decided that we should move up the steep hill where the trees offered more protection. We quickly packed up our small camp and repitched the tent. Arnold and I had just crawled inside when the rain began to hammer down, hitting the canvas like a cascade of pebbles. It continued all night. Our paddlers, who had stayed closer to the river, moved up the bank too as the water was rising.

Arnold had grown up in a similar environment to this in Sarawak, so I felt safe with him. Knowing that he carried a gun also helped to reassure me. I reasoned that, if he showed no sign of fear from the noises outside, then there was nothing to be afraid of. But all the same, when a roar like a tiger's woke me from my half-sleep, I began to recite psalms! It was a long night.

Looking out of the tent the next morning I was amazed to find that the river had almost reached us, having risen about 25 feet in the night. We were stranded. We moved further into the forest where the men cut down trees to make a clearing, and rigged up a shelter. Arnold made a table and chairs and a bed for each of us so that we would not have to sleep on the ground. He was so capable, gifted in all sorts of ways. I knew it was unfair to compare them, but as I tried to picture the clergy I knew back home in Newcastle turning their hand to a spot of alfresco carpentry, I failed miserably.

Arnold and I went fishing while the men went off to hunt. Back in our camp we lay on our tree-trunk beds and he told me stories about his life as a boy in the forest. He was born in a longhouse in a village called Entanggor in Sarawak.

'I had a younger brother I had to keep an eye on, and an older sister, who was also my cousin but had been adopted by my parents. We did what children did – following the adults around, learning how to fish and hunt, and working in the fields. You quickly learn how to survive.'

After the village primary school he went to St Thomas's Secondary School in Kuching, and from there joined the House of the Epiphany theological college and became a priest.

I realized what a huge step this had been for Arnold, and felt my admiration for him grow even more. He was a youthful-looking man, whose small stature belied his strength, yet I tended to think of him as older than me, for he seemed so capable, so wise. It was therefore a surprise many years later to discover that he was born in 1931, and was a year and a half my junior.

We had never spent so much time in each other's company, and it felt natural to speak to each other about our lives. I told him about my own childhood in Amble vicarage. He listened, wide-eyed.

'A high stone wall went all the way round the house and garden. A door in the wall led into the church junior school, which is where I went until I was eleven and moved to the grammar school in a bigger town nearby. My brother Joe went to boarding school, and I missed him a lot, as I didn't have many friends in Amble. I learned to enjoy my own company. During the war, people in the country took in evacuees from the cities, and as our house was so large we ended up with several – my grandmother and aunt, a teacher and three of her pupils, and an Army officer.'

'Wendy,' Arnold interrupted, 'you too were living in a sort of longhouse!'

He cut some saplings and showed me how we could suck them for liquid, and pointed out edible plants and insects. The rain started again and we had to take refuge in the tent. It leaked, and we got soaked. Arnold lay with the chalice on his chest to collect rainwater for us to drink.

The next day the river had risen higher still. As there was no hope of continuing upriver in our tiny boat, Arnold decided we should paddle back to Karamuak where we might be able to borrow a boat with an engine to take us back to Tongud, where we could pick up our own outboard motor and start out again.

After breakfast we struck camp and were swept downstream. It was a most strange experience; we were level with the treetops and kept having to duck to avoid branches. A journey that had taken a whole day to complete in the opposite direction now took us just an hour and a half, and we were there before noon. But there was no motorboat to borrow there. We dried our dripping belongings, and I bathed and wrote to Joan.

A little later I found Arnold feverish and gave him Nivaquine. We clearly weren't going to be going anywhere else that day. We slept on the floor in a room in the shop. A rat eyed me from the corner as I prepared to lie down, and was joined by another. I clapped my hands and they disappeared. Not long after settling down I heard them return. Strangely, I was less bothered by them than I was by the giant moths that had found their way into the boarding house in Sandakan, or the cicadas that boomeranged from one side of the room to the other.

The men, who had gone out hunting, disturbed my hardwon sleep when they returned much later. When I awoke properly just before daylight they were lying beside us, along with a pig they had shot with Arnold's gun.

Our men set off for Tongud to bring back our outboard motor. Arnold's temperature was still high, and I felt the beginnings of enteritis. We spent two days in that room as we waited for the men to return and Arnold to get better, eating some of the meat they had left us. I attended to some patients, draining two abscesses and extracting a tooth. The rest of the time I read *She* magazine, which I had stuffed in my bag at the last minute. It was both surreal and comforting to read recipe ideas for dinner parties and suggestions for what to wear for these occasions as I sat on the floor in my squalid surroundings, regularly inspected by the resident rat family. Later I moved my bedding outside and slept on the balcony, hearing the calls of orangutans in the night.

I wondered what my parents would think if they could see me, if they would be shocked to see the way their only daughter was living. Mum was already trying to help. She had been alarmed to learn that we had no way of reaching Sandakan quickly in an emergency, and had decided to take it upon herself to raise money to buy us a faster boat. There was no stopping Mum when she had a bee in her bonnet, and she had already organized an 'at home' day in the vicarage.

It was Ascension Day when the men returned with *Bintang Epiphany*. Arnold and I had begun the day with Mass in our little room, accompanied by the radio and the sound of Chinese voices singing. At the end of it came the BBC News – clipped English tones that could have been coming from the next room and made everything sound so reasonable! And suddenly I no longer felt quite so isolated.

Arnold was much better, so we retraced our route up the River Karamuak in the outboard, towing the smaller boat. Apart from stopping to eat, we travelled all day, making camp on a pebbly bit of shore. One of our paddlers shot a pig and the men dissected it at the riverside, keeping the liver and kidneys for our meal and smoking the rest of it on a platform they built over the fire.

Journey to Telupid: Wendy in a *perhau*, with *Bintang Epiphany* behind

I mentioned to Arnold that I hoped no pigs would come near us in the night and he replied that pigs were the least of our worries.

'Somewhere like this, I am more afraid of elephants and snakes,' he said.

I didn't like the idea of Arnold being afraid of anything. He proceeded to tell me about all the other animals that lived in this habitat: deer, honey bears, orangutans, rhinoceros, wild cattle, monkeys and something similar to a tiger.

He enjoyed teasing me, and I knew there was a twinkle in his eye as he spoke. But that night I begged him to stop. I could hear all those animals getting closer and was sure they would somehow know that I was the lily-livered foreigner and make me their target!

I awoke early, too hot and sticky to stay in my sleeping bag. We had porridge and tea and left in the outboard

motor. The river that had shocked us with its force just a few days earlier was soon too shallow for our larger boat, so we transferred to the perhau and continued slowly. As the river became narrower the trees met over our heads, providing us with welcome shade and occasional glimpses of blue sky and sunshine. It was all very beautiful and peaceful, and in those moments I could think of no place I would rather be.

At times I felt like an explorer crossing uncharted territory. As I made fires with wood – with no punk or paper to help get them started! – I gave thanks for my years as a Girl Guide. I told Arnold how the captain at the First Warkworth Company I had belonged to had also been the county camp advisor, so I had received excellent training in woodcraft and survival skills. Later I had been captain of St George's Guides, taking my group of city girls camping in the Northumberland countryside.

When Sunday came, I helped Arnold build an altar and we celebrated Mass, watched, rather suspiciously, by our men.

The river grew wider, the view opened out, and we saw mountains soaring ahead.

We left our canoe hidden on the riverbank and continued our journey on foot, soaping our shoes, socks and legs to guard against leeches.

Arnold showed me how to recognize the footmarks of different animals and how to tell how recent they were.

'These are from a pig and those are wild cattle.'

A little later he cried, 'Over there! Elephants!' But by the time I looked where he was pointing I could only see the swaying branches they had left behind.

It was so hot that we stopped every 20 minutes to rest. The path was overgrown and had obviously not been used for some time. One afternoon we lost Arnold for over an hour when he went ahead with his gun, and I felt anxious until I saw him again, the plaintive cry of a bird making me more agitated. He told me it had been a peacock.

Arnold made us a bed out of logs, with a sloping roof of leaves to keep off the rain, and we slept on it, side by side, like an old married couple.

'We're still alive,' I commented the next morning.

'Of course. Why would we not be?'

'Oh, I don't know – snakes, bears, marauding elephants. Exhaustion. You didn't mention any of this in that article I read in the *Borneo Chronicle*!'

'You worry too much, Wendy,' laughed Arnold.

We were walking at times along the old Japanese trail, but it was so overgrown that the men struggled to know which way to go. I averted my eyes when they stopped to bathe in the nude, right in front of me, but decided that the time had come to ditch my bra!

At 3.30 p.m. one afternoon, ten days after we had set off, we emerged from the trees and found a perhau waiting for us. After a short paddle we arrived at a timber camp where, on an incline in a clearing, we were confronted by the surreal sight of a very large British man – who appeared to be the manager of the operation – sitting at a table in a comfortable chair as if he had been expecting us at that very moment.

'Come and join me,' he said. 'You're lucky to catch me. Tomorrow the camp is moving three miles into the forest.'

He called to an assistant, and a few minutes later we were drinking tea and eating scones, butter and jam.

We left our jovial host and a few miles farther on reached our destination of Telupid, only to discover that the OT, the man we had come all this way to see, had gone away for five days.

One of the villagers was seriously ill with pneumonia, and I attended to him before the deputy OT showed us round and introduced us to the Dusun teacher. We were pleased to see that the school buildings were in good repair, with kajang walls and atap roofs.

Telupid was beautiful. I kept stopping what I was doing to admire the mountains all around, made more dramatic by the constantly changing clouds that sat heavily on top of them.

That night we slept in the school boarding house. I was relieved to be inside as it sounded as if elephants were trying to break down the building. Arnold pointed out the prints of buffalo the next morning. Patients began arriving at 6.30 a.m. I had to use ethyl chloride spray as a general anaesthetic on one, to remove an embedded wisdom tooth.

I managed a few moments of solitude and some glorious bathing at midday before checking on the pneumonia

Wendy holds a clinic and gives healthcare advice during her travels

patient, who was much improved. Then it was back to my makeshift clinic until it was dark.

That evening we attended a meeting in the school with three local OTs and the Dusun teacher. In a very short time they agreed to hand over the existing school to our mission the following January. They promised to erect more buildings, including a dispensary and a house, and signed letters of agreement for the Education Officer and Frank. All our efforts had been worth it. Arnold and I cooked a meal and went to bed very late.

As we headed off the next day on our long trip back to Tongud, I thanked God for keeping me going, surviving as I was on so little sleep, the gluey heat and humidity sucking every bit of energy out of me.

6

Rags and riches

June to July 1960

It felt like coming home to get back to Tongud.

'I've missed you!' said Joan. 'And it looks as if other people are missing you too.'

She pointed to a pile of letters waiting for me. There were 23. Several of these were from my mother (my most prolific letter-writer while I was away), but there were also two from Rhoda (who often included women's magazines and pull-out supplements she thought would interest me), one from my brother Joe, and the rest from a mixture of school and nursing friends, friends from church and other supporters.

I was less happy to find that rats had eaten holes in my mosquito net. As I didn't fancy succumbing to one of the many mosquito-borne diseases myself, one of my first jobs was to mend it as best I could.

I found Ulor in his room in the dispensary, where his family had been taking care of him. He was playing with a wind-up toy car which was tied with string to one of the legs of his bed so that he could pull it back towards him. The incision had healed nicely and he could move his leg. I told him I would have him up and walking again soon.

The dispensary looked dirty and neglected and I set to work getting it shipshape. I was proud of my standards of cleanliness, though clearly I had to accept certain limitations in light of my unusual circumstances. Back at Charing Cross Hospital, when I had started on the wards for the first time after three months in the classroom, I had been given the task of cleaning the toilets. Being pleased with my efforts, I was horrified to be summoned by the strict ward sister and asked to follow her back to the lavatories, whereupon she rubbed her finger along the surface of one of the cubicle doors and, glaring at me, showed me the dust that had collected on it. After that, through a mixture of fear (she was a formidable woman) and determination, there was no one better than me at keeping lavatories, bedpans, urinals and vomit bowls scrupulously clean!

As I worked, two patients arrived after a long walk from a kampong deep in the forest. The woman's left leg was grotesquely swollen, her foot almost hidden under the misshapen calf. I recognized elephantiasis, a disease caused by a parasitic worm that is spread by mosquitoes. There was little I could do other than give her antibiotics to stem any infection, advise her on hygiene and recommend the elevation of her swollen leg. She would probably not be the only person in her village suffering from this, but to stop it spreading I would need to treat the whole community. Her companion had acute arthritis of the right shoulder following an abscess. His shoulder had an open area the size of an (old) English penny, covered with a thin membrane, close to the axilla. I would have liked to excise this and stitch it up, but the local anaesthetic I had ordered a couple of weeks earlier had still not arrived. I told them both to come back later, not knowing if they would do so.

I was more than ready for a dip as Joan and I set off to our bathing spot. It was always the best time of the day. The water was pleasantly warm – nothing like the rivers I had plunged into on hikes in Northumberland, where the icy water took your breath away – yet it was still refreshing. Problems and worries washed away when I was in the river. Events that had seemed shocking or dangerous when they occurred managed to craft themselves into entertaining stories. All the same, Joan was horrified when I told her about the trip to Telupid.

'I wonder if Frank really knew what he was doing, sending you there,' she tutted. 'It's all well and good him sitting in the rectory in Sandakan and coming up with these ideas, but carrying them out is another matter.'

Feeling defensive on Frank's behalf, I suggested that he was unlikely to ask me to do anything he wouldn't be prepared to do himself.

'Hmmm, but still, you're hardly made for this climate, Wendy. I think Frank has to understand that. It's different for Arnold – he grew up in the jungle! But even he found it hard going by the sound of things.'

'I suppose my problem is I can't say no to a challenge,' I said.

Joan laughed. 'I can see that. I think we're similar there. We both know what we want, and won't let anyone or anything get in our way.' She began to clamber out on to the muddy bank. 'And what I want now is some of that Fray Bentos pie. I bet you didn't have anything as delicious as that in Telupid!'

I had to admit that I hadn't.

As usual, we were hot and sweaty again by the time we had walked back to the house.

Frank was about to return to the UK on furlough, and as he was going to be visiting churches and community groups back home to tell them about the mission in Tongud, he wanted to take with him a recording of me talking about my work. He had also promised to visit my parents and my friends at St George's, Jesmond. A group at my old church, now known as the Tongud 80, had pledged to each give half a crown (today, equivalent to about £3) a week for the mission, which was going to allow me to buy better and faster-acting drugs than the ones currently at my disposal. An even larger group of supporters received my regular newsletters, which were typed up and printed by the secretary of local housebuilder William Leech, a friend of my mother, and sent all over the UK. I knew that I was on the prayer list of many churches across the country, and I felt huge gratitude for that.

'As you have seen from my letters, I don't even pretend to be brave,' I said in the recording. 'I find a lot of things here a challenge, but the support you give me keeps me going in my difficult hours.'

There was interference on the line, and we had to redo it a few times, but eventually Frank was happy with the result.

Soon after Frank's departure, I heard from Father Briggs, who was standing in for him at St Michael's Church, that Sister Christina and Novice Ginyam were preparing to visit me in Tongud. I radioed back that evening with a shopping list for them.

The next day I woke up with a sore throat and a head-ache, but a surprise visitor took my mind off things. Martin Wilson, the young man who had been one of the party that had accompanied us to Tongud, was making his way back to Lamag from Penungah, where he had been supervising census work. He gave Joan and me a hand in the dispensary and the classroom, and stayed for lunch. He told us he would be returning to the UK soon in order to start university in the autumn, so this might be our last meeting. He took our letters with him when he left, including a mammoth one I had written home about the trip to Telupid – 18 pages, and yet I felt I could have written even more!

After he had gone, Joan discovered two bottles of perfume inside a toilet roll in a parcel of provisions he had brought us, along with a note saying, 'Wendy and Joan, I do hope the smell is bearable! It's been terrific to meet you both. Keep up the good work! Martin.'

Arnold teased us, saying that it might have been a hint!

I had started getting Ulor on his feet again. He held tightly to me the first time, and I could see his trepidation as he gingerly put the leg that had caused him such pain on to

Wendy helps Ulor take his first walk outdoors, watched by his family

the ground. We walked just a few yards, but increased the distance every day, and he grew more confident each time. He looked as pleased with himself as a toddler taking his very first steps.

As I kept an eye on my patient, and the dispensary continued to be busy, about a dozen of the boys in the boarding house went down with coughs and colds. Joan said she would give me a hand.

'You didn't realize you were going to be a nurse as well, did you?' I teased her, as she helped me to rub chests, administer cough medicine and add drops of eucalyptus oil to hankies (made from some of the material that had been in the package sent by SPG).

'You're right. And you didn't realize you were going to be a doctor!'

We were both drawing on talents that we hadn't known we possessed.

A letter arrived from my mother telling me they had raised £150 from her 'at home' day. I was delighted, and wished I had known earlier so that I could have thanked everyone in my recording. I had also been sent enough money from my friends at St George's to buy a kerosene fridge for the dispensary. A fridge would allow me to stock medicines I currently had no means of storing – the only antibiotic at my disposal being procaine penicillin, which had to be injected into a muscle and was not the easiest thing to use. I would be able to carry out vaccination programmes for the government and immunize the pupils against childhood diseases.

Now that I was getting into the swing of my new job, I had other ideas that I was keen to put into action. I wanted to teach hygiene and preventative healthcare: so many of the illnesses I saw were caused or exacerbated by the way people lived. I had made a start on this by speaking to the pupils about handwashing and guarding food from flies, reasoning that if I could get through to them, the simple measures I proposed might be passed on to their parents. I also wanted to start an antenatal programme and, mindful of the high rate of neonatal mortality, to deliver babies in the dispensary.

When I shared my thoughts with Arnold he said that he admired me, but warned that the plan could backfire. 'The people here are very superstitious. If a mother or baby should die in the dispensary it will be seen as an omen and you may find that no one will want to set foot in there again.'

Well, I would have to deal with that if and when the time came. For now, I was giddy with all my plans, though a voice inside my head kept telling me to be realistic and that there were only so many things I could hope to achieve – not least because I was the only person to carry them out.

Talk of my having an assistant in the dispensary, which had been voiced from time to time, seemed to have evaporated, but Arnold had recently come up with the idea of asking one of the schoolgirls, Helena, if she might like to give me a hand. Helena was a bright, mature girl, the oldest of the school's four female pupils and the daughter of the *Towkay* (boss), the Chinese owner of the *kedai* (shop) in Tongud. It was agreed that she would help me for a few hours a week, and I found her a willing, capable assistant. It was particularly useful having her to translate the different Dusun dialects when my patients spoke no Malay.

With Helena's help, I translated into Malay and Dusun some of the health posters I had brought with me, and I made some new ones of my own. I also posted the dispensary's opening hours on the door: 7.30 a.m. to 12.30 p.m. and 2 p.m. to 4 p.m. Monday to Saturday, allowing time for lunch and a rest at the hottest part of the day. However, as few people wore watches or had Western concepts of time, people had a habit of turning up at any hour. I even used their own method of timekeeping myself for some purposes, telling patients with tablets to take three times a day to take one when the sun was rising, one when it was overhead, and one when it was setting.

I was determined to see my plans through, though most of them would have to wait until after the summer break, which I would be spending in Sandakan and Jesselton.

My sore throat had turned into tonsillitis. My tonsils, large and angry-looking, were covered in septic spots. Arnold and I had been due to take a short trip together but had to postpone it. I dosed myself with sulphatriad and hoped it would do the trick.

While I was feeling rotten, I fell through the bamboo slats in the passage leading to the kitchen. I was cut and bruised, but mainly I felt stupid. Andrew came to repair the floor that same day with some old planks.

'Why don't I make you a bookshelf while I'm here,' he suggested, looking at my large library.

That cheered me up instantly. He put it above the desk in the living room where I sat every evening to write my diary under the light of the oil lamp. There is nothing like displaying your books to make a place feel like home, I thought! *Flying Doctor Calling* went up beside *Dr No*, *Annapurna* and C. S. Lewis's *The Four Loves*, while a pile of Rhoda's *She* and *Woman's Own* magazines acted as a bookend.

Wendy house: the living room, with furniture made by Andrew Kiri

I heard a clamour of excited voices and saw a group of boys who had been in Tangkulap returning with our post and another consignment of SPG bale. Right behind them, being competently carried on the shoulders of four boys, was my fridge!

'I could hardly believe my eyes, after all this time!' I wrote to everyone at St George's later. 'It had been taken out of its box to come upriver in the launch, and travelled the last lap in a dugout canoe!'

I watched with my heart in my mouth until it was in its place in the dispensary, whereupon I washed it out and lit the flame. Then I began to unpack the bale, which I hoped would be more useful than the last lot, which, apart from the hanky material, had contained knitted woollen items that would only rot in this climate, as well as being far too hot to wear. I felt guilty, as I knew it had been sent with the best intentions by people at home wanting to help. At least we had all had a laugh, as Arnold wrapped the giggling boys in coloured scarves so that they looked ready to face the chilly streets of Newcastle!

The bale this time consisted mainly of rags and pieces of material, towels and cot covers, along with needles and some medical instruments. I could give some of the better pieces of material to the locals to make clothes, and Joan would probably be able to make something ingenious with it. I chose some to make cushion covers for our living room, and there was a pretty blue-and-white check that would make a nice pair of curtains for my bedroom.

But there was a problem, too – there was a lot to store and I had very few shelves. Another job for Andrew, I thought. I was certainly keeping him busy.

I had patients all day, but whenever I had a moment I went back to see if the fridge was cold, before deciding that it was like the watched pot that doesn't boil. I took some photos of a Tongud family leaving the dispensary – the three children wearing some of the bright SPG cottons, clutching their milk and soap that had been donated by Unicef.

Before going to bed I checked the fridge again. It was still warm. I had expected it to take a while, but surely this was too long. I wondered if it had been damaged in transit. It was a disappointing thought.

I rushed over to check again as soon as I was up. No change. I turned it up to full light and went back after Mass. To my relief I found that it was beginning to get cold. I put in the tetanus antitoxin and a tray of water. A few hours later, ice was starting to form in the tray.

As we waited to hear news of the progress of Sister Christina and Novice Ginyam so that we could send some boys down to meet them, we received a message that Mr Hunt, the DO (District Officer), would be arriving later that day. By the time it grew dark he had still not arrived so we knew not to expect him until the next day. Mr Hunt and his party turned up as we were having breakfast. I would grow used to visits from passing government officials, missionaries, timber merchants and various prospectors over the next two years, and even though a visit meant extra work for us – more mouths to feed, sleeping arrangements to be made – it always provided a welcome interlude. I think those travelling along the Kinabatangan needing a place to break the journey knew that in Tongud they were guaranteed a friendly welcome from Arnold and the rest of us, so we probably received more visitors because of that.

I told Mr Hunt that my mother was planning to come to visit me the following year, something she had confirmed in her last letter, and that I was very much looking forward to it.

'But how will she cope?' asked one of his men, putting down his cup of tea and looking most concerned.

I pictured my determined, capable mother. 'The same as the rest of us,' I replied.

My tonsils were still sore but I was feeling slightly better when we heard that the sisters had reached Bilit. Three days later I was starting to grow anxious, then we heard that they were at Tangkulap, and sent some boys to meet them.

'What happened? I've been worried about you!' I cried as I helped them off the boat.

It turned out they had been waiting in Tangkulap for two days, but the person responsible for letting us know had failed to pass on the message. It wasn't an uncommon occurrence.

The next day the sisters came to see the dispensary in action. Nalang had been bitten by a wild pig. He had two huge gashes in his right forearm which needed stitching, but I was still waiting for the local anaesthetic. Hoping it would turn up very soon, I asked him to stay in the dispensary so that I could operate as soon as it arrived.

In the afternoon Joan and I took our visitors for a walk round the village, and we stopped at the kedai. The Towkay wasn't there, so Helena served us tea. The pupils could exchange *damar* gum – a resin obtained from tapping the trees – for school supplies in the kedai, which also sold some basic goods and foodstuff, though its stock was very limited.

'Don't you get unbearably hot?' Joan asked our friends, as they sat sipping their drinks, looking surprisingly comfortable in their habits. Sister Christina's habit and headdress were dark, though her novice's were a cooler-looking white. Joan and I changed into sarongs when we finished work for the day, ditching our bras and anything else that wasn't strictly necessary, and still I sometimes felt I would die in the heat.

'Funnily enough, long loose clothes are cooler than shorts and T-shirts,' said Sister Christina.

I wiped some sweat from my brow. 'Really?'

'You'll be missing this when you get back to Newcastle, Wendy,' Joan teased.

'Never!' I said. And I meant it. 'I'll never complain about the British weather again.'

Later Arnold took us for a walk up the hill, behind the mission buildings, where we had views of the river and hills and the fields of tapioca. After the hot climb, we were more than ready for our bathe when Joan and I led the sisters to the river. We had had a lot of overnight rain – the jamban had been flooded that morning – and the water was higher than usual and very muddy.

'We'll take you to the beach when you come to stay with us,' said Sister Christina, looking at our favourite spot rather dubiously.

'It's different every time we swim,' I said to her. 'Too deep, too shallow or sometimes just right. But – oh! – it's always blissful!' And the sisters laughed as Joan and I plunged in.

Dinner that night was rice and pig – funny how we now used some of the locals' words! – followed by apple crunch and custard. As we were gathered together in our small sitting room, I felt more comfortable with these new friends than I had felt with anyone for a long time. It was like being back at St George's, surrounded by like-minded people – people with whom I could be myself without having to worry about what I said.

'When I was younger I wanted to be a nun,' I confided. 'My parents were a bit surprised, but after being very protective of me when I was a child, they let me make my own decisions as I got older.'

'What made you want to?' asked Joan.

'I think I imagined a peaceful, meditative life, being at one with myself and nature.'

'And what happened?'

'I went to live in a convent in Middlesbrough, and got quite a shock. It was hard work! I realized pretty quickly it wasn't for me.'

'I don't think I can see you as a nun,' said Joan.

'God knew what He wanted for you,' said Sister Christina. 'You trusted Him and He showed you the way.'

I knew she was right. I had found my vocation, though it tested me severely at times.

The sisters left, and Ulor, now walking almost without a limp, returned to his kampong. I would miss him, but he promised to come back to see us. Arnold developed a fever, which put a stop to the trip we had rescheduled. Though I didn't let on, I was mightily relieved about this as it coincided with my time of the month. It was all very well Arnold giving me a few days' notice for these expeditions, but he didn't have some of the extra problems we women had to contend with! Suffering from period pains and worrying about changing sanitary dressings wasn't much fun in a canoe or the middle of the jungle.

In Tongud there was no such thing as a postman. Letters, goods, medicines and schoolbooks arrived only when there was someone to bring them. Sometimes, if someone was travelling the whole distance, they made their way upriver from the post office in Sandakan quickly; at other times they went from one place to another, languishing here or there for days at a time until passing river traffic could bring them on the final stretch of the journey. The local anaesthetic arrived one day in the care of the indigenous chief, and I was too relieved to question why it had taken so long. I was now able to repair Nalang's lacerated arm.

With Joan and Andrew to assist (Arnold was still unwell, though I wondered if the thought of the task had kept him in bed longer!), I got Nalang on to the operating table. I administered morphia and, half an hour later, infiltrated the area with Xylotox. Joan took photos of me using the scalpel to remove excess granulated tissue that was protruding.

All was going well when suddenly blood began to spurt from Nalang's arm with great force. I realized to my horror

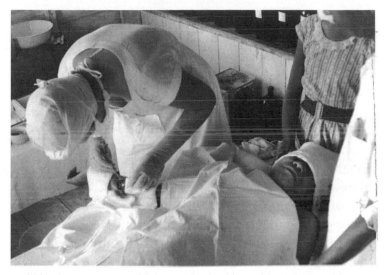

Wendy operates on Nalang, who had been bitten by a wild pig

that I had cut an artery. While Joan pressed firmly with a pad, I used some rubber tubing as a tourniquet, which An drew held in place. Stay calm, I was saying to myself. Behave logically. Don't panic. But inside, my stomach was churning, my heart pounding so loudly I was sure everyone else could hear it, my mouth so dry I could hardly speak. I spent ages searching for the artery so that I could tie it off with catgut. Each time I loosened the tourniquet to see if it had been tied, more blood rushed out. I was growing more and more desperate, and my panic must have been obvious to my assistants. I pictured Nalang dying here on the table and remembered what Arnold had told me about the locals and their superstitions. Blow it! After everything I had achieved so far and the trust I was building up with the people, this was going to be a serious setback. I pictured myself traipsing off to see my patients on foot from now on – that's if they hadn't all resorted to seeing Tutu the local witch doctor, or Dalila the medicine woman.

After a few more attempts at tying off the artery, I released the tourniquet and was relieved to see the flow had ceased. But I was still worried that it might loosen and Nalang would haemorrhage. As I attempted to suture, he began to bleed again.

After some consideration I decided to leave the wound, dress it and accompany my patient to hospital in Sandakan immediately. I hastily packed the dressings and drugs I thought I would need, and Joan went to pack some provisions. Andrew rigged up a stretcher with two planks of wood and some of the boys carried Nalang down to *Bintang Epiphany*, a *gobang* (canoe) that had an outboard motor. Joan came with us so that she could hold the tourniquet should my patient haemorrhage, and two of the older boys were our skippers.

We left Tongud at 2.30 p.m. and arrived at Calambadan at 11 p.m. The place was all shut up. Joan and I slept on the jetty – or tried to sleep – alongside the gobang so that we could observe Nalang. I had administered pethidine and he was sleeping soundly.

At 6 a.m. we went looking for the manager to see if we could use the speedboat, but it had been promised to someone else that morning. With no other option, we carried on downriver, hoping to be able to borrow a boat from another timber camp along the way.

After two hours we reached Balag camp – and discovered that the manager was in Sandakan with the speedboat. Later that morning, at another timber camp, the manager said he was going to Sandakan the next day and that we were welcome to accompany him, but he was unable to go sooner. We were getting desperate now. Hearing a speedboat on the water, we frantically waved it down. It was Mr Hunt, the DO, on his way to Lamag. After hearing our tale, he allowed us to use his boat and said that he would find another means of getting there.

We left at 1 p.m., the skipper and Joan in the front, me in the back squatting beside my patient. There was no room to move, and I was too anxious to read, as Joan was doing. I didn't relish the thought of seven hours in this position.

It began to rain. The boat had no shelter so I tried to cover Nalang with a lilo and a sheet of canvas. We reached the Trusan – the name given to the area of water between the river mouth and the open sea – in the dark. The water was very shallow and the channel narrow, so that the vegetation almost met at our sides.

The engine cut out and refused to restart. Joan held a torch as the skipper paddled; sometimes he had to get out and pull the boat. Joan said we might have to spend the night here and told me to look out for crocodiles, who favoured these salty, shallow waters.

When Joan dropped the torch over the side, I thought it was gone for good, but the skipper jumped in after it and, seeing it shining in the shallows, managed to retrieve it. It all happened too quickly for us to question how sensible this move was.

We were travelling very slowly as it was difficult to see, and the last thing we wanted was to damage the boat by crashing into something. It wasn't uncommon to come across stray logs from the timber camps floating in the water. The waterway here was like a maze, and in the dark even our knowledgeable guide sometimes seemed unsure which route to take. He continued to retry the engine, without success. It began to look as if the safest option would be to spend the night in this sinister place, the air thick with mosquitoes.

Then, on the umpteenth attempt, the engine started. Our guide seemed more confident about the route, and we began to make progress again. As the water was swept back we saw luminous green phosphorescence, which was very beautiful. All the time Nalang slept, oblivious to our troubles.

I was relieved when we reached the sea, and even more so when we saw the lights of Sandakan twinkling on the other side of the bay. The water was calm, and we arrived safely in town at 9 p.m. An hour later, we had taken Nalang to hospital by taxi and were sipping gin and tonics with Father Briggs in the rectory.

7

A hard chair and a bucket

July to August 1960

'Miss Livingstone, I presume?' said Mr Hunt as he shook my hand.

'Do I look that unkempt?' I asked him, laughing.

'Not at all. But you are a pioneer, Wendy, in the truest sense. When people talk about Tongud they always mention the two young Western women, working so selflessly in a place few would dare travel to.'

'You make us sound like romantic figures,' I said. 'I'm not sure it feels like that when you are actually living there.' I looked at Arnold. 'Here is the real pioneer,' I said.

We had landed in Sandakan for the summer vacation. After our emergency trip, Joan and I had returned to Tongud to find Arnold just recovered from his fever and Andrew running the school single-handedly.

Joan had to stay on for a little longer, but I had packed up my things and closed the dispensary, and Arnold and I sailed back to Sandakan together.

After our short meeting with the DO we loaded our *barang* (luggage) into a taxi and went to St Monica's School, where Sister Christina showed me to the best room in the boarding house. It had a huge window, with a glorious view over the town and to the islands beyond. I showered and unpacked, after reading the letters that were waiting for me from home. After lunch I was ordered to rest, but there was so much to think about that I found it almost impossible, and instead

Sister
Christina
reads
to her
novices

occupied my time writing a to-do list and starting a letter to my parents. I also wrote a quick one to Joan to tell her we had arrived safely. After tea at 3.30 p.m. – how civilized life in town was! – Sister Christina and I drove to the hospital. We passed cyclists holding umbrellas that would protect them from sun or rain, and other cars, though no one ever appeared to be in a hurry. I saw Nalang and was relieved to see that he was recovering well. Then I went to talk to Dr Christiansen about my septic tonsils. A nurse gave me an injection of penicillin and asked me to come back the next day for another.

I was woken the next morning by Sister Christina coming into the room with a breakfast tray. Orange juice, toast and marmalade, and a pot of tea.

'I'll get up and give you a hand as soon as I've finished,' I said after I'd thanked her, but she shook her head in protest.

'It's the first day of your holiday and you've had a hectic time. Let me spoil you for a little while.'

I stayed in bed, drinking tea and rereading my letters until it was 10 a.m. It was hard to believe that I'd spent the previous night on the floor of the gobang, lying side by side with Arnold so that his mosquito net (I'd forgotten mine) could cover us both, the mission boatman, Majang, sleeping at our feet! I had kept my knees bent all night so as not to kick him.

I went back to the hospital for a second injection then had a lazy afternoon, writing letters to Lawrence and Bishop Wong, whom I would be seeing soon in Jesselton. Arnold came for supper and we played Scrabble with the sisters until it was bedtime. I enjoyed these evenings, with their shared games and conversation. I didn't remember playing games with my parents when I lived at home. Instead, while I sat reading, they would fill their evenings diligently making proggy mats – a north-eastern craft in which old sacks and recycled fabric (or, in their case, strips of wool) are turned into sturdy but attractive rugs.

The next few days passed in a pleasant routine. I wrote letters. I did some errands for Sister Christina. I made lemonade using my mother's recipe, which everyone enjoyed. I played tennis with Father Briggs, Barbara Beaumont and John Brummell, the Australian principal of St Michael's Secondary School. It was terribly hot for tennis, but on the cloudier days it was just about bearable. The sisters, Father Briggs and I carried on our studies of Malay, and played Scrabble before bed.

But I was still unwell. When it was clear that my tonsils were not responding to treatment, Dr Christiansen arranged for me to see a German ear, nose and throat doctor in the town as there was no such specialist at Sandakan's hospital. Dr Sychta frowned when he saw my tonsils and declared them to be in a poor state. As the penicillin and the sulpha drugs were clearly not working, he told me I would need to come back for a tonsillectomy, but first an abscess on the left tonsil would have to be dealt with. He gave me some tablets which he said would make me feel better in a few days, and made an appointment for me to return in a week's time.

I was quite dejected after this. I had certainly not envisaged needing surgery myself while I was in Borneo. I felt weak, and angry with myself. Furthermore, I knew nothing about Dr Sychta and, while I trusted Dr Christiansen and his recommendation, I was unhappy about putting my health into the hands of a man I had only just met. And yet I felt there was no alternative.

Back in my room, Sister Christina brought me a lemon and honey drink and gently listened to me pour out my woes. Her eyes behind her spectacles were full of love and concern. She was a rock to me, and I don't know what I would have done without her.

We had some visitors for coffee the next day – a teacher and parishioner from All Saints' Church, Jesselton, with her mother, who had come out to visit her. I told them that mine was hoping to do the same, and listened to their stories about the places they had visited together.

'We've heard all about you from Lawrence Jones,' said the young woman, as I looked at their photos.

'Really?'

'He admires you so much. Says you really are the pluckiest woman he knows!'

On the day of my operation I painted my nails. Rhoda would be proud, I thought with a smile, as I pictured my immaculate aunt, who had been the manager of Wetherall of Bond Street. The day before, Joan had trimmed my hair. Very thick and curly, it was the bane of my life, and I felt like a new woman whenever it was newly cropped. When it was done, Joan sat down and I dressed the septic leech bites on her foot.

'They're almost better now. So whatever happens to me tomorrow, you won't need me.'

Joan widened her eyes at me in annoyance. 'Don't talk like that!'

But I was worried about this operation. I had spent the past few days preparing for it and catching up with overdue jobs, which included writing letters I owed and sorting out my photos, putting captions on the ones I was sending home to my parents.

Sister Christina accompanied me to Dr Sychta's surgery for my 4.30 appointment. Ten minutes later I was sitting on a hard wooden chair, holding a bucket on my lap. Sister Christina sat facing me, a few feet away. Dr Sychta injected the local anaesthetic around each tonsil before bursting the abscess behind the left one. Pus poured out. I retched into the bucket. In my head I recited the twenty-third psalm. I finished, and began it again. The doctor began to cut away each tonsil in turn; old scars on the left one made it more adherent. I heard his concentrated breathing, his sighs.

'The Lord is my shepherd,' I began again. 'I shall not want. He maketh me to lie down in—'

I retched again.

I caught Sister Christina's eye. She was white. I wondered if this experience might even be worse for her than it was for me. I felt sorry for her. I felt sorry for myself. I questioned the wisdom of what was happening. If people back home could see me now!

'He leadeth me beside the still waters.'

It was done. Dr Sychta put a large nylon stitch in each side and a pack of gauze.

He and Sister Christina led me to the ambulance that I had booked to take me to hospital to recuperate, knowing the danger of haemorrhaging after a tonsillectomy. Sister saw me into bed before leaving. I was in a first-class single room with my own bathroom, but the curtain at the window was not only too short but also too narrow, so the men on the balcony of the adjoining room could see straight inside if they so wished. However, I was in no state to worry about that. The pain was terrible; the pethidine I had been given on arrival was having little effect. I longed to drift off into the numbness of a long sleep, but sleep refused to come.

Father Briggs arrived at 7.30 and offered to write a letter home for me, but somehow I scribbled one myself and asked him to post it. An hour or so later Dr Christiansen appeared and gave me more pethidine, which relieved the pain slightly but still didn't bring the oblivion I longed for. I lay there, aware of each passing minute, until at 3 a.m., as the pain intensified again, I rang the bell and was given another 100mg. This time I slept for a couple of hours, but the morning routine began all too soon and brought me back into wakefulness and suffering.

It was agony every time I had to swallow. All I could manage were a few sips of liquid. I dozed on and off, but never for long. In a room opposite, a child cried constantly for his mother. In the early evening Sister Christina and Novice Ginyam arrived, just as Dr Sychta turned up, so they said they would return later. I sat on a stool in the bathroom as the doctor removed the stitches and the gauze. As I was getting back into bed, wondering if I might manage to sleep for a while, Barbara, Joan and two teachers from St Monica's arrived with sweets, books and flowers. I was gratified by their love and care, but it was an effort to write down my answers to their questions, for speaking was impossible, and I really just wanted to be left alone. The sisters came back, as promised but, seeing all the visitors, said they would return the next day.

'Dr Sychta says you can have a normal diet today,' said the nurse who brought me my breakfast tray. On it was juice, eggs and toast. I could still barely swallow but managed to mash the egg to a pulp and force about half of it down. In the afternoon Sister Christina and Joan arrived, and I did manage to croak a few words. Cyril Innes, a British doctor at the hospital, and his wife, Phoebe, whom I had met socially, popped in, bringing ice cream, and Father Briggs arrived in the evening and we said Compline together.

I knew that my recovery would take a while, and so it proved. But as soon as I felt I wasn't going to be a burden to my friends, I returned to the boarding house.

I had just about enough voice to give a talk and presentation about our work with Joan in St Michael's church hall. Frank's congregation were our most long-standing supporters and I was determined not to let them down. The following day, Joan and I flew to Jesselton, where we had a week of engagements. From my seat in the front of the plane there was nothing to see but jungle and muddy rivers winding through it. As we neared Jesselton the terrain became more mountainous and we passed close to Mount Kinabalu, more than 13,000 feet high.

There was quite a party to meet us: Bishop and Mrs Wong, Mr Lai, who was churchwarden of All Saints' Church and chairman of the town board, Lawrence Jones, and several other expats and officials. Like Sandakan, Jesselton had been heavily bombed in the last war and new, modern buildings were everywhere.

All Saints' Church – completed in 1959 on a site opposite the old one – was a striking building, painted white with a red roof. As we had coffee and cake in the rectory where we were staying, we were bombarded with invitations, including one to a function at the Governor of North Borneo's residence, and another to a dance. I wrote straight to Sister

Christina asking her to send my silk dress, stockings and smart sandals.

Inevitably, the subject of my tonsillectomy came up. Everyone looked aghast.

'You poor girl,' said Mrs Wong, patting my hand. 'You have been very brave. I hope everyone took care of you as well as you do of them.'

Lawrence looked annoyed. 'You ought to have been flown to Singapore or Hong Kong. I don't know what SPG were thinking, sending you to some back-street doctor.'

'Oh, I don't think he was that. He's a specialist – the only one in town. SPG didn't hear about it in time to do anything, so I can't blame them.'

Everyone had an opinion. I wished they would stop talking about it in the end. I was starting to feel that I had been rather foolish in going ahead with the operation.

We were treated like royalty over the next few days. We had no need to worry about how we were going to get from one place to another as Lawrence seemed only too glad to drive us, or to arrange taxis when he was unable to do so. Joan commented on how attentive he was, and I agreed that he was the most thoughtful, generous man.

On the first day of the new term, Joan and I joined Bishop and Mrs Wong at All Saints' School for their first assembly. We sat on the stage and were applauded when the bishop introduced us. Then Joan and I went to each classroom to talk for a few minutes, and I said a special thank you to the pupils, having learnt that each class was making a small monthly donation to pay for an assistant to help me in the dispensary. After that it was back to the rectory to get ready for the governor's lunch. I wore my Wetherall silk dress, pearls, my twenty-first-birthday ring and Chanel perfume. Looking at myself in the mirror, I felt like a different person from Sister Grey in her plain white uniform, or off-duty Wendy in her sarong and flip-flops!

Mr Lai picked us up and took us to Government House, where we were welcomed by His Excellency the Governor, and Lady Goode. The other guests included two British MPs, an American judge and the wife of a local doctor. I embarrassed myself by sprinkling too much ginger on my starter of papaya balls, which gave me a coughing fit. The Labour MP passed me a glass of water. When the chicken course arrived, the red wine I had taken only a few sips of was whisked away and replaced with a white. Wise to the process, I made sure to drink all of my next glass before it happened again!

After lunch we returned to the rectory to change, then Lawrence collected us and took us to the beach to bathe. Later he and I went for a walk at Likas Bay, where we sat and watched the sun set.

Lawrence told me he had been married, but it hadn't worked out. He asked if I had left anyone special behind in Newcastle.

I shook my head. I had had a few boyfriends, of course. One of them, a houseman on the ward while I was doing my training, had even come to stay in the vicarage in Stannington, but it wasn't meant to be.

'There's a big group of us who socialize at my church in Newcastle,' I told him. 'Both sexes. It's often easier like that.'

'Perhaps.' Lawrence looked at me, then fixed his gaze on the horizon. 'But nothing beats a true companion.'

When I went to collect the post that evening, there was a letter from home. I kicked off my shoes and stretched out on my bed to read it. The postal system often felt like

A letter from
home

a small miracle – a slim piece of paper, finding its way from my mother's desk across countless miles, handled by who knew how many people, yet arriving more or less in the same condition as when it left her hands! Sometimes letters took as little as a week to reach me. I read the letter, then read it again, before catching up with my diary. When I had finished it was almost midnight and I gratefully got into bed.

On another day of back-to-back functions, Lawrence offered to run us to the beach before our fundraising tea party in the rectory garden. He knew I couldn't resist a swim in the warm sea, though he always went for a walk while I swam. Joan changed her mind at the last minute and said she would rather stay in and finish a skirt she was sewing, so in the end it was just the two of us. As I swam I planned in my head some of the talk I was going to give at the tea party, for there had been so little time to think about it. But after meeting and speaking to so many people during the course of our stay, I felt that the words would probably take care of themselves.

At the rectory, Joan and I were introduced to the 80 guests as they arrived. I felt that my smile had become rather forced by the time I had finished shaking so many hands and saying how pleased I was to make everyone's acquaintance. We sat down to tea, scones and cake, before Joan and I gave our talk. Later we found more than $250 (Malaya and British Borneo dollars) in the collection box for the Interior Mission. To celebrate, Bishop Wong took us to a hotel for a meal, over which we discussed what we felt was our greatest need for the mission – a decent boat with an outboard motor that could be used as an ambulance. With the money Mum had raised earlier, along with recent donations, we were now in a position to make a purchase.

Lawrence had to visit a census office in Kota Belud, about 40 miles north of Jesselton, and invited me to go with him. I was glad to sit back and not have to be anywhere in a hurry. In the past few days Joan and I had given more talks, been interviewed for the press and radio, and joined some of the expat crowd for picnics on the beach. I had also been to the local hospital where I had met the colony matron, Miss Waites, someone I would get to know even better in the months ahead.

The drive took us along roads with beautiful views of the hills and of Mount Kinabalu. In the valleys of wet padi, bright green shoots were vivid in reddish muddy water. It was the season for planting and we saw water buffaloes at work and wallowing in the mud at the roadside.

As I looked out of the car window I must have been singing to myself, for Lawrence said suddenly, 'Don't stop!'

I laughed. 'I would sing some of the *Messiah* for you, but I can't reach the high notes any more. Not since my tonsillectomy.'

Lawrence told me I should be patient. He played the organ, and suggested we practise together in church sometime.

We had lunch in Kota Belud Rest House, a modern one-storey building, before visiting the census office and watching the figures being gathered in. The census for Sarawak had been taken on 15 June, and one for North Borneo two months later.

'Your head must be full of numbers, Lawrence,' I said, teasingly.

'Oh, yes, numbers and other things!'

On our return trip we got stuck on a muddy mountain road. I was growing anxious about making it back for the parish dance at the Community Centre, but some men came to help and managed to push us out.

'I can't believe we've crammed so much into these past few days,' said Joan, as I zipped her into her long dress that evening. 'I think going back to Tongud is going to be as good as a rest.'

Back in Sandakan, Joan had just a couple of days to prepare to travel back for the start of the new term. As I saw her and Andrew off on a well-loaded *Malaikat*, one of the ladies from St Michael's, who had been at our talk, came rushing down to the quayside.

'We were all horrified when you told us you had no fresh eggs,' she said breathlessly.

She handed Joan a roll of wire netting to make a run, and two cages containing six pullets and a cock.

8

The mission cat

September to December 1960

Several things delayed my return to Tongud. My throat was painful again and I could see an abscess on the right side. I went to see Dr Sychta, who said it was unusual to have complications after a tonsillectomy, gave me a local anaesthetic and cut it out. Sister Christina sent me to bed when I got back to the boarding house, but no sooner was I up and about than it was her turn to need me, and I found myself ferrying her to see Dr Innes at the hospital in the school's Hillman Husky, as none of the sisters or novices could drive.

Sister Christina needed an operation, and she shocked Dr Innes by requesting that she be treated as a third-class patient. He made a joke about everyone at the hospital getting third-class treatment whether they asked for it or not, but was sufficiently alarmed to send us to Sister Barr, who said it was most irregular.

'I don't believe a European has ever gone third class in the colony before,' she announced, looking from me to Sister Christina, as if waiting for one of us to admit that it was all a joke.

'There's always a first time,' said Sister Christina, sounding more determined than I had ever heard her.

Sister Barr added that she didn't think Sister Christina would be able to stand the food. (I couldn't help thinking that the food would be the least of her worries!)

Seeing that she was getting nowhere with her patient, and deciding it was easier to pass the matter on to someone else, Sister Barr said that she would have to see what Dr Christiansen thought.

I felt that this was surely a matter for Sister Christina to decide, and no one else, but thought it best to stay quiet. Over the next few days, neither Father Briggs nor the sisters could talk Sister Christina out of the idea.

Swallowing was agony. I returned to Dr Sychta, who passed it off lightly and said I was well enough to return to Tongud. 'But come back in a few months and I'll cut more away, if necessary.'

Sister Christina and Father Briggs were unhappy about this and insisted I get a second opinion. As it happened, they knew just the man.

In the centre of Sandakan, Dr Christopher Willis ran the Christian Book Room clinic. Dr Willis had been born in China to missionary parents and had trained as a doctor in Canada. Before arriving in Borneo he had also worked in Bermuda and Singapore, and now operated as a sort of independent GP in Sandakan, dispensing his healing to whoever needed it and often refusing the offer of payment. He was known for his ability to diagnose almost any disease with the simplest of tests and equipment, and as he had no interest in personal wealth or status, his opinions were always trusted.

Dr Willis examined my throat, declared it to be ulcerated and gave me some tablets to suck. He said I should not go back to the mission until it had cleared up. I was more relieved to hear this than I cared to admit.

The doctor and I got on well from the start, and when I told him about my work and how I was hoping to learn more about the tropical diseases I encountered, he invited me to use his laboratory whenever I needed to. I would spend a lot of my free time bent over a microscope there over the next two years.

A few days later, while I was writing to Lawrence and Rhoda, Sister Christina came into my room looking distressed. She was holding a cable that had just arrived from her Reverend Mother in Devon.

'She insists I go on a first-class ward,' she told me tearfully.

I wasn't surprised. I indicated that she should sit down on the bed so we could talk properly. While she usually took great pleasure in our chats together, this time she shook her head.

'Reverend Mother is right,' I told her. 'So many people need you and rely on you. There is no point in making things hard for yourself. Why, you will only increase the chance of having to stay in hospital longer, getting frustrated over all the things you should be doing here!'

But she remained upset, and her gloomy mood filtered through to us all that day.

Later, Dr Willis advised Sister Christina that her operation was not urgent, and added, to my alarm, that he would not recommend anyone having an operation in Sandakan unless it was absolutely necessary. I only wished I had met him earlier!

I left Sandakan to return to Tongud on 24 October 1960, which happened to be St Raphael's Day. This felt like a good sign. The new mission boat, which would be in operation in the new year and had been made possible thanks to the generous donation of a *jungkung* (flat-bottomed canoe) by Dr Christiansen and a 25 hp engine Joan and I had purchased with the donations from friends in Borneo, the UK and Australia, was to be called *Malaikat Raphael*. *Malaikat* was Malay for 'angel' or 'messenger', and St Raphael was the patron saint of travellers, nurses, physicians and medical workers. Before coming to Borneo I would have put myself in one or perhaps two of those categories, yet now, I thought, all four of them might describe me!

I departed in our usual boat, *Malaikat*, towing a smaller one lent to us by Mr Hunt for the upper reaches of the river, as our gobang, *Bintang Epiphany*, was too rotten to use. Father Briggs and two of the sisters came to see me off, and I waved to them until they were out of sight. We were a small crew this time – just me and Majang, the skipper, who was a Dayak, like Arnold and Andrew, and one of the original members of the mission. But today we also had a new member of the Tongud mission, Jeremy the kitten, whom Arnold had asked me to bring.

Jeremy was very frightened, and I tried to calm him down by showing him round the boat. I let him wander round by himself, and not long after that he disappeared. I took over the steering as we went through the Trusan, so that Majang could eat. Then Majang went under the floorboards to look for Jeremy, who had now been gone for several hours, and he reappeared with the trembling creature. I spent the rest of the day holding him in the cradle-like security of my sarong, which was awkward whenever I wanted to move out of the sun or take over the steering, but it was the only way I could get him to settle.

The river often became too shallow for bigger boats beyond Bilit, but there was no such problem today. We stayed at a timber camp where we were awoken at 4 a.m. by a gong summoning the workers, followed soon after by the radio blaring out. The manager's wife had a baby monkey with a blue face and hands that she was feeding from a bottle.

Jeremy was frightened by the boat's engine when we set off, but by the time we had arrived at Camp Pin, he was relaxed and playful.

After being given coffee at the camp I was offered a ride into the forest to see the men at work. A contraption that had been built using a motorcycle engine took me three miles along a wooden track. I watched the men sawing huge logs and rolling them on to wheels for transporting. Later they would be placed on rafts and sailed downriver to Sandakan, a common sight on our journeys. On the way back to the wharf the chain on my unusual mode of transport broke just as it started raining, whereupon my guide presented me with a banana-leaf umbrella.

I saw my first crocodile between Camp Pin and Lamag and was surprised by how excited I felt. It was lying on the river bank, huge and dark brown. Majang steered the boat nearer so that I could take a photo, but it slid into the water and disappeared.

By the last night of our six-day journey, Jeremy was sharing my mosquito net. He would wake me in the mornings by washing my hair and my ears.

News of my return to Tongud quickly spread, and I was back in the dispensary within a couple of hours of my return. Helena came to help me for a few hours the next day as I unpacked boxes of medicines and put up new posters. I went to visit Fatimah, a girl who was very ill with malaria. Having not yet unpacked my mosquito net, I resolved to do so as soon as I was back in my room.

One of the four female pupils at the school, Lily, had begun to help Joan and me in the house with some simple cleaning duties. Joan and I were very fond of her. She was about seven years old and shy, but with a mischievous sense of humour, and she enjoyed our company, quietly observing us as we went about our routines. She showed me the curtain that divided my bedroom from the living room. It had been half-eaten by rats while I was away. I pointed to Jeremy, snoozing happily in the corner, and mimed him pouncing on a rat, which she found very funny. He had caught his first mouse, a tiny thing, in my room the night before, and had played with it until it escaped through the slatted floor. I hoped he would earn his keep and find some bigger prey, but he was still a little thing himself.

I had no sooner got back when Arnold told me we were going to be travelling again. Puru-Tawai was just a few hours upriver from Tongud, and necessitated only one night away from home. I might not have remembered this trip among all the longer and more dangerous trips we made if it hadn't been for one thing. After holding a clinic in the home of the OT, where we distributed dried milk, salt and soap, I was asked to visit a man who was having trouble walking. I found

The Dusun house at Puru-Tawai

my patient with a swollen knee, but attending to him was his emaciated 16-year-old daughter. I was shocked when I saw Simin. Her clavicle, sternum and ribs jutted alarmingly out of her tiny frame; my thumb and index finger encircled her twig-like arms and even her lower legs, with room to spare.

I sat down beside her and took her hand. 'You must go to hospital,' I said in Malay.

She smiled at me.

I looked at Arnold for his help to translate, and said, more firmly, 'You must go to Sandakan where they have a hospital for tuberculosis. Do you know what that is? It's an infection of the lungs. It can be treated, but you might need to stay there for several months.'

Arnold spoke to her father, who appeared to understand, but we both felt that there would be more chance of him complying if the headman understood the urgency of the situation. Back at his home we spoke to the OT, who promised to take swift action.

I thought about Simin as we travelled back to Tongud. It had upset me to see this pretty young girl wasting away in front of everyone's eyes, with no one having thought to suggest that she might need the attentions of the clinic. Was it because she had no boils, abscesses or disfigurement? Was it because she could walk and move her limbs? Was it her uncomplaining nature? I was angry with her father and with everyone else in the village who had allowed her to reach this pitiful state, and because it was only by chance that I had seen her. Arnold tried to appease me by telling me that all that mattered was that she would now get the treatment she needed, but it took me a long time to calm down.

In the evenings now, after finishing my dispensary book work, I often wrote letters with records playing in the background. My battery-operated record player hadn't worked at first but had recently been repaired in Sandakan. *South Pacific* was my current favourite. Sometimes I forgot what I was supposed to be doing and lost myself in the music.

'I'm gonna wash that man right outa my hair,' I sang, much to Joan's amusement. Of course she wanted to know whom I was thinking of as I sang, but I assured her that there was no special person playing on my mind.

I sounded and looked happy. But while I was working to the very best of my abilities, while I was sociable with Arnold, Andrew and Joan and enjoyed jokes with Helena, Lily and the schoolboys, inside I felt irritable. My ill health. The wearing climate. Too much to do and not enough time to do it. Too little time for myself.

My new plans were starting to take shape, and just this week two pregnant women had turned up in my clinic, the first takers for my antenatal programme.

Helena had carried out a survey for me of Tongud and its inhabitants – 87 adults, 145 children including 44 boarders, 36 occupied houses – and drawn a simple map showing where everyone lived. Using this, I had begun a programme of health-visiting every house.

But had I bitten off more than I could chew? As if to rub salt in the wound, I had just learnt from Bishop Nigel that the assistant I had been promised was not able to come after all. It was back to square one.

A few nights later, everything changed when I made my first confession since arriving in Tongud. It was dark beside the confessional so Arnold lit a candle. As I confessed my sins and Arnold pronounced God's absolution, a feeling of peace and tranquillity washed over me. I felt like a different person. My mood lifted considerably from that point. Even though every night as I sat and wrote my diary I felt exhausted – sometimes exasperated too – I also felt contented.

Helena continued to be a great help, and after the morning's clinic she accompanied me upriver one day to visit a woman called Naria, who was too sick to come to us. She had a temperature of 105, and pains in her loins and abdomen. The next day her temperature was down slightly but her abdomen was distended and she remained very sick. Helena did her best to translate, but I was at a loss for a diagnosis. Back home, after attending to a long line of patients, I pored through my medical books. Typhoid fever? Pyelitis?

Over the radio the next morning I asked Sister Christina if she could find me a doctor to speak to that afternoon for advice. Arnold, Joan and Helena came with me when I visited Naria again, taking a bedpan and some other equipment. The river was flooded and very fast, and we felt vulnerable in our tiny canoe with its 15 hp engine. I found my patient much the same, with a temperature of 101. I catheterized her and gave her an enema, pethidine and Chloromycetin. She was continually spitting and covered with flies. I told her family that I would like to take her to the dispensary for proper clinical care, which I couldn't provide at home. Moreover, with the river in flood I couldn't safely continue to visit her. The reply was that they had arranged a mameow to start that evening, so Naria would be unable to come for a couple of days at least. I had no choice but to leave her, and asked them to bring her when they wanted our medicine.

There was no one on the end of the radio that afternoon, but the next day was Sunday, and after Mass I tuned in to Sandakan where, to my relief, Dr Christiansen was waiting for me. For a change, reception was good at both ends. He complimented me on my treatment of Naria so far, and gave advice on drugs and dosage.

I continued to worry about her, while a new patient began to take up a lot of my time. I first saw Moses in one of the *tamu* (guest) houses where he had arrived after a difficult journey from Puru-Tawai. He had been brought by his son, Joel, one of our pupils. It was common now for boys to bring their relatives to the dispensary; people who might never have seen a nurse or doctor in their life were now, thanks to the trust built up through the education of their children, voluntarily leaving their homes and feeling confident that they were coming to a safe place.

Moses had a very swollen and painful knee. I read up on TB knee, then decided it might be bursitis. I admitted him as an inpatient. Joel would stay, too, and cook for him.

I heard nothing more of Naria, but later that day saw a frame covered in large banana leaves being floated upriver, which I guessed were for her mameow. I wanted to help her but it seemed that this time I wasn't going to be given the opportunity.

The next morning I attempted to aspirate Moses' knee, without success. I suggested he might go to Sandakan for treatment, but he refused to consider it. As his temperature was down and his knee slightly less swollen, I didn't press him on the matter.

It was an unusually quiet November day in the dispensary as I repacked and sorted the travelling medicines case. When I had finished I moved on to the cupboard, and was removing lint rolls from a wooden box when a rat jumped out at me. I called for Jeremy, who went straight into the box and unearthed a nest of four tiny rats, each one an inch long, which he ate, but the big rat got away.

My new companion and pest controller was proving useful, but there were disadvantages too. I had been woken one night by the most frightful din as Jeremy and some other creature came leaping through my bedroom window, hissing at each other, until eventually all went quiet. The next day there were bloodstains all over one of my uniforms, which no amount of scrubbing could get rid of.

Joan and Arnold had gone out for the day. At about the time they were due back I heard an engine, and saw two strange men coming up the path from the river. Mr Meijer was a Dutch forestry officer from Sandakan and the other man was his skipper. Mr Meijer said he had asked Father Briggs to let us know that they would like to stay for a few days, but the message hadn't got through. I wondered if Arnold could put them up, but his house was leaking, so I found them a space in the store room in the dispensary to sleep.

Bill Meijer was interesting company. He had spent most of the previous decade in Indonesia as a lecturer and professor of botany. Now he was employed by the Forestry Department of North Borneo and had turned his attention to tropical forest botany. The next day he took Joan into the jungle with him and they returned laden with leaves and vegetable matter, which he proceeded to catalogue. He told us he was going climbing for a few days to find more indigenous plants, but would be returning.

I discovered two empty bottles of kerosene on the ground. I was puzzled, until I remembered that Joel, the son of my inpatient, had gone to his kampong for the day. In the dispensary kitchen lay dirty plates with evidence of fish on them, and a stocktake revealed several tins of fish missing from the store. I almost stumbled over five of them lying in the grass, a few feet away, a couple unopened, along with a half-full tin of Nestlé cream.

When Joel returned that afternoon I asked him about the missing kerosene and food, with Arnold acting as translator. He denied taking anything, and his father denied having been given any of the food. Moses blamed two other pupils, who were duly summoned and admitted to the theft of the fish, but also implicated Joel. They were obviously all guilty. Giving him the tablets he would need to continue taking, I told Moses he could leave the dispensary and move into a tamu house. I felt very sad as I watched him and Joel wandering off down the hill, clutching their pathetic bits of belongings, and I felt sorry for Arnold, who thought of the pupils as his own children – indeed, they called him 'Fadder', their pronunciation of 'father', and he was like a father to them all. He couldn't speak to me at first, and went up the hill for a walk. Later he told me that low-level stealing was common; the boys would take his clothes to wash – singlets, hankies, and last week his favourite shirt – and he wouldn't see them again.

I worried that I had been too severe. What was I doing worrying about small amounts of food when these people had so little? But our food and our kerosene had to last us. I felt that I could almost accept the stealing, but not the lying about it.

One evening, after Arnold had cooked a special meal for Joan, Andrew and me, he complained of a pain in his right side that he said had come and gone over many years.

'Where does it hurt?' I asked him.

I watched his fingers move over the tender area.

'Too much work!' joked Andrew.

'Yes, time for a holiday!' Arnold agreed. He often spent whole days and nights with the boys in the forest, bringing back wood that would be turned into posts to build the chapel – we were still using a room in the school as our place of worship – or atap for our leaking roofs. If he wasn't doing that, or teaching, he was showing the boys how to prepare terraces on the hillside for planting rubber.

'Pain in the RIF,' I said, half to myself.

I could hear Sister Tutor back at Charing Cross. 'And what might that mean, Nurse Grey?'

'A grumbling appendix, Sister?'

I looked at him firmly. 'Please, Arnold, do not have appendicitis out here! Wait until we're somewhere sensible!'

It was the first day of December, and my first patient of the day was Lily, with acute colicky abdominal pain she had been experiencing for the past 24 hours. She yelled and screamed whenever the attacks occurred, upsetting anyone who heard her. I gave her pethidine to relieve the agony, and kept her in for observation and treatment. Her mother stayed with her. I found things to do in the dispensary all afternoon and evening so that I didn't have to leave her, then, when it was getting late, I went back to the house to write my diary and get ready for bed. Lily started screaming again at about ten o'clock, so I went back and gave her pethidine and something to help her sleep.

The screaming started again the next morning. A bowel movement in which she passed a roundworm did not alleviate the pain.

After lunch, Mr Meijer returned from his trip with more leaves and vegetation. In the evening I had just finished a letter to Lawrence and gone to bed when I heard Lily's cries and went back to attend to her. Worry about Lily played on my mind, and I took a sleeping tablet to help me rest.

Bill Meijer had a disturbed night, too, thanks to having to share the dispensary with my young patient. He suggested that she set off for Sandakan in his gobang and 18 hp engine and transfer to a speedboat from Pintasan. I was grateful for his offer, but first there was the tricky matter of gaining permission from her family. Lily's father was away and his three wives were not happy about making the decision without him. I told them I thought Lily would die if she stayed. Mr Meijer tried to help me, and when the women continued to waver, called OT Harun, our headman, and asked him to speak to them in Dusun, which did the trick. Mr Meijer carried Lily down to the boat, where I prepared a bed with a woollen blanket.

I held the hand of my little helper. 'Don't worry, Lily, you're going to be fine. The doctors and nurses in Sandakan are my friends and they'll take care of you.'

I wasn't sure how much she understood, but though she was in too much pain to smile, her eyes looked hopeful.

The boatman promised to look after Lily and deliver her safely to hospital. I watched anxiously as the boat sped off down the river.

Sometimes it wasn't medicine that was needed, just a little understanding. A boy of 15 was brought in, ringworm covering his entire body. Ringworm has nothing to do with worms, but is a fungal infection that produces ring-shaped rashes on the skin. It was common there, where people wore no shoes, and I could treat it. But there was another problem.

'He is stupid,' Helena told me.

'What do you mean he is stupid?' I chided her.

'That is what they say,' she replied, pointing to his parents.

His father gave his own impression of what he meant, then demonstrated stabbing motions at his own chest.

'He sometimes tries to kill his father with a knife,' said Helena.

I sat down and tried to speak to the boy, using a mixture of Malay and sign language. It took a while, but we slowly began to understand each other. Over the course of the next half hour I discovered he had been deaf and dumb since birth. He could work, and was intelligent, but people often laughed at him, which made him angry – and sometimes violent. He responded to the efforts Helena and I made to engage him, and seemed so pleased when I gave him some magazines to take away, and asked him to come back to see me sometime.

Just before I closed the dispensary that day someone dropped in to say hello. It was Ulor, proudly showing me his knee and telling me that he could now run and hunt as well as he did before.

9

A schoolboy surgeon

December 1960 to May 1961

Lily returned to Tongud in good health just before Joan and I set off to Sandakan for Christmas. Roundworms had caused an intestinal blockage. She was full of tales of her exciting time in hospital, of the uniformed staff and the ward routine, and of the cars and bikes she had seen in the streets of the town. It was a sharp reminder to Joan and me of the things we took for granted.

'I hope you didn't want to stay there, Lily,' I said, pretending to be upset. 'And when we've missed you so much!'

She grinned and hugged me.

We sailed with a pig that Arnold had bought from Lily's father that he wanted us to sell for a good price on the way, to make money for the mission. I wasn't exactly happy about having a pig on board, but felt I could hardly object. At least Jeremy, who I was taking with me, was a seasoned sailor now and I didn't have to worry about him this time.

The Christmas holiday began with the school nativity play, and was followed by hospital and parish parties and dinner invitations. A highlight of the holiday was meeting Bruce Sandilands, the pioneer who had ensured that Frank had left the relative comfort of Sandakan and gone into the interior to see a different Borneo. Perhaps it was a surprise to me to discover a humble, softly spoken English gentleman, who had been born in 1921 at the foot of the South Downs, though was proud of his Scottish ancestry. However, I was

A welcome break: Wendy and Joan relax on one of their holidays

learning not to be surprised by anyone or anything in Borneo. On New Year's Eve, Joan and I joined Bruce and other guests for dinner at Dr Christiansen's. Four glasses of champagne kept me awake for the club dance, where we sang 'Auld Lang Syne' and Joan and I were kissed by all the men.

I also started getting to know better Tony and Dorothy Meyer, a British couple I had met on an earlier visit, who had become generous benefactors of the mission. Mrs Meyer was proud of her beautiful garden, and I loved spending time in it. She had many different types of orchid, and could name them all, but what stopped me in my tracks when I first saw it was her New Guinea creeper, which boasted trailing clusters of bright-orange flowers.

In the hospital laboratory and the Christian Book Room clinic, I gained experience using the microscope. Dr Christiansen and Dr Willis showed me how to detect the malaria parasite in a patient's blood and tubercle bacilli in sputum using the Ziehl-Neelsen stain. These were skills that would serve me well in Tongud.

Joan and I got a shock when we walked back into our house a month later. It looked derelict, with thick dust covering every surface, cobwebs hanging down and a damp, musty smell. We set to work cleaning it up. The dispensary was in a slightly better state, but the glass funnel of the fridge was broken. I went to get a spare and found that the box of four I'd been given were the wrong size. With a sinking feeling I realized I faced the prospect of all of the tuberculin and BCG being wasted. I tried patching the funnel with adhesive strapping, but it melted off. I had another go with a piece of foil and some wire. It seemed to do the trick, but I couldn't see the flame to regulate it. I left it, hoping for the best.

Joan put a smile on my face, popping in to show me an armful of nine-inch-long cucumbers. She and some of the boys had planted them six weeks earlier, just before our departure for Sandakan, and they were flourishing in the warm, wet soil.

One of my first patients was a 16-year-old girl who had given birth a month earlier and hadn't walked since. I saw Palima in the OT's house. She had a large, raised, tense area, like an abscess, on her right midriff; lactation had failed and her infant was in a pathetic state and continually crying. I gave the baby Lactogen and glucose and the mother some painkillers and admitted them both the next day so that I could operate on Palima. It was the first time I was using Pentothal – a new general anaesthetic at my disposal – without supervision, and I was rather nervous.

It was a quick-acting drug, but also quick to wear off, so only usable for a short procedure. Palima was very thin and it was difficult to find a vein for the Pentothal. After several attempts I decided it was impossible and gave her morphine and ethyl chloride, but she became hysterical. I tried her veins again and was eventually successful. She was unconscious in 30 seconds. I incised the abscess and thick pus poured out. A bit of catheter served as a drainage tube and I fixed it with a nylon suture.

It was now a full-time job keeping an eye on Palima and taking care of feeds and nappy changes for the baby, but I managed to leave them to attend a quick meeting at Arnold's house, which was also attended by OT Harun. It had been decided that his son, Tanguran, would start work the next day as my temporary assistant.

The last time I had seen Tanguran was just before Christmas when I had been called late at night by the OT and Ederiss, an intelligent boy of about 15 who helped with the younger pupils. They told me Tanguran had been bitten by a scorpion. I had set off to the home of the OT, only to find myself being led to the river and paddled to a house where a *berunsai* (social celebration) was taking place. In a room swarming with people and where the intense heat felt suffocating, I found Tanguran slumped in a corner, in a state of shock, his arm swollen from his hand to his elbow. I noticed Ederiss swiftly remove the traditional medicine in the form of leaves that had been placed beside him. Tanguran responded to my reassurance and the treatment I gave him, and though I was reluctant to leave him there, he made a speedy recovery.

I was pleased to have Tanguran as my assistant. He seemed keen to learn, had a pleasant personality and spoke reasonable English. As his wardrobe consisted of just one pair of shorts, three shirts and no footwear, I advanced him

$10 of his monthly pay of $60 to buy more shorts and some canvas shoes.

He watched me and asked sensible questions as I showed Palima and the baby's grandmother how to prepare feeds. They were both much better, and Palima was moving around cautiously. She fed and bathed her child for the first time and seemed thrilled with the whole process.

I was crossing the compound one morning when Dalila, the medicine woman, called out to me, '*Jangan marah!*' ('Don't be angry!') I discovered that a patient I had been treating, and who was now well on the mend, was taking the extra precaution of having a *berubat* (traditional medicine).

'I'm not angry with you, Dalila,' I replied. 'But you know I don't believe your medicine can work on its own.'

Although we held opposing views on the subject, I felt that Dalila and I had reached some sort of compromise.

I had recently been called to the house of a Muslim, a short way upriver, to see a young girl who I was told had been crying with abdominal pain. I found her with a distended abdomen, Dalila at her side. I went back for my enema equipment and when I returned she had been curtained off in a corner, as I had requested. That was when I learned she was Dalila's own daughter, a 12-year-old who had just become engaged to a boy of the same age. The enema produced a good result and the girl brightened up. I felt I must be making progress if the medicine woman herself had asked for me.

Even Tutu, the witch doctor, had summoned me on one occasion, when a woman was taken ill in the OT's house, causing Ederiss to announce to everyone who was there,

'When people are very ill they need Sister Grey. The kampong medicine is no good for serious cases!'

I climbed the hill for a different perspective and a chance to contemplate. Down in our clearing in the forest, there was little to see other than neighbouring buildings and the muddy path between them. At this vantage point, with views of the hills and the river, I found it easier to empty my mind if I needed to, or to ponder difficult problems. In a few months' time Mum would be here with me. While it still seemed a long way off, I knew that with so much going on, the time would be here before I knew it.

Funny to think of Mum in Tongud! Though she had been overseas to visit my brother Joe in Canada, and we had holidayed in Europe together, it was hard to picture her out here. She was an Englishwoman of her time, a product – as was my father – of a boarding-school education and Victorian parents. Joe and I had both learned from them the stiff upper lip and to conceal our emotions. She had married my father at the age of 28 after a five-year engagement, during which he was at theological college and not permitted to marry. Now, as a long-time vicar's wife and Mothers' Union supremo, she was an organizer, an extrovert and a great hostess, and would be more than capable of dealing with whatever experiences came her way in Tongud. Our relationship had grown warmer over the years; it was not as close as it might have been considering I was her only daughter, but we got on better now than we had ever done and I knew she was proud of what I was doing. Still, she was a dominant woman, and it would be a testing time for us both to be in each other's company for 24 hours a day over the course of ten weeks.

After he had been helping me for a week, Tanguran turned up for work exhausted. He told me he was finding it difficult to sleep in his house as there was so much going on – currently the preparations for a Muslim wedding. He continued to do as he was asked but his enthusiasm had gone.

The next morning he didn't turn up at all. I heard there had been singing and dancing in his house until 6 a.m. I sent him a message and, when he still didn't arrive, Andrew and I went to find him. He was still sleeping and complained of a headache. I gave him aspirin and asked him to come to work as soon as he was ready as the dispensary was crowded. He didn't show up. It was a long day, made more tedious as I had to keep leaving my patients to relight the temperamental fridge.

Tanguran did not appear the next day either. Just as I was contemplating paying him another visit, Arnold came to tell me that Tanguran had written to tell him that he found the work too hard and the pay too little. As if this wasn't bad enough, Andrew told me that Helena was finding dispensary duties too much with her schoolwork and wouldn't be returning either.

I looked at the people still waiting to be seen and felt quite despondent.

At dinner that night, Arnold told me that he knew a young man who might be interested in helping. Though I smiled and listened, I didn't hold out much hope.

Wendy diagnoses diseases
from stool and sputum
specimens

I was trying to stain some sputum from a woman with suspected TB. I had no Ziehl-Neelsen stain so tried with car-
bolfuchsin, but it was no good and the light was poor so I
decided to wait until the next day. When I did I found tuber-
cles. It was my first discovery in Tongud with a microscope,
and I felt both pride in myself and sorrow for my patient. I
told her she must go to the TB hospital in Sandakan, but she
seemed reluctant.

Using Andrew as a translator, I asked her why she didn't
want to go.

'She is worried about her children and her husband,'
Andrew told me.

'But TB is infectious,' I said, as calmly as I could, hoping I
was masking the frustration I was feeling. 'She might pass it
on to them. She will be a better wife and mother if she puts
her own health first on this occasion.'

He told her what I had said and she promised to speak to
her husband.

I had made progress in attracting patients to the dispensary, but hospital continued to be an alien concept to many
of the people here, and its distance – more than 300 miles

away, in a town most of them had never visited, for few had ever left the interior – was another barrier.

The young man Arnold had mentioned appeared for work one Monday morning in February. I liked the look of Samuel – though hadn't I thought the same of Tanguran? But in his spotless white shirt that was tucked into a dark pair of shorts, and with his socks and shoes, he presented a professional image from the start. I allowed myself the hope that this time it would work out. Despite his youth, 18-year-old Samuel was a married man, and his wife, Larnia, was in the final trimester of her pregnancy.

'Perhaps Larnia can have her baby here in the dispensary,' I said, optimistically.

Samuel smiled and nodded, but I thought his eyes betrayed some doubt. I knew that his mother was a kampong midwife, so wondered if that might cause future conflict.

Samuel had been working for me for a week when Arnold turned up at our house late one night to say that he thought a young man was dying. Seeing how worried he looked, I followed him to one of the tamu houses. Sixteen-year-old Patrick, who had been brought from Malagatan Besar, a kampong high in the hills, had left school the year before and was now married. He presented a shocking sight: semi-comatose, in acute pain and groaning. His face and neck were huge, he was unable to move his jaw or open his mouth and his neck was rigid. Tetanus was my first thought, but when I managed to look in his mouth I noticed three lower right molars missing, and pus and blood exuding. It appeared to be a submaxillary abscess, and I was in no doubt that this required special surgical care. However, I still spent several hours that night swotting up on oral and maxillofacial surgery as an extra precaution.

This was the first emergency trip for the new boat, *Malaikat Raphael*, the 30 x 4 feet flat-bottomed canoe we had brought back with us from Sandakan after Christmas. We set off as soon as it was light, with Andrew driving and Samuel as lookout. It was difficult holding my balance to prepare injections and keep Patrick hydrated when going through rapids, and my legs and back ached from some of the awkward positions I had to adopt in the cramped space.

On more than one occasion I thought that Patrick might die before we arrived, so slow and erratic was his breathing. Fortunately, *Malaikat Raphael* went well, and by travelling for 12 hours each day, stopping only for fuel and to sleep, we reached the mouth of the river after two days.

We had been given refreshments and lent more petrol by our friend Ray Kelly at the Rivers Estate en route, and he had tried to make contact with Sandakan to let them know we were coming and ask for a launch to tow us over the bay. However, no boat awaited us. As the water looked calm, we set off unaccompanied, only to find large waves coming at us from the side. Andrew drove fast, and it was exciting at first to be lifted right up by the waves, but as the sea got rougher I was only too aware that our little boat was not meant for these conditions and that we might not make it. As I often did in times of fear, I sang 'The Lord is my shepherd' to myself, and tried to put on a brave face for the others. It was one of my most terrifying journeys. We reached the wharf in half an hour, buffeted, soaked and relieved.

Patrick was sleeping when I went to see him in hospital the next day and looked very peaceful. It was my birthday, and so I found myself in the delightful situation of opening presents surrounded by my friends in the boarding house. Sister Christina gave me her rosary; the novices gave me some

Wendy, Arnold (in hat) and schoolchildren with mission boat
Malaikat and (below) *Malaikat Raphael*, the ambulance *jungkung*

flowers. Barbara gave me *The Music Man* record and Jean a set of Chinese bowls. Later the staff of St Monica's came for a tea party and I received more gifts before collecting mail from home from the post office. Perhaps the best present of all was when Mrs Meyer turned up with a cheque to cover the cost of the petrol for the trip.

The journey back was notable for one thing in particular. In Camp Pin, where we spent a night, I was shown to the guest room which, despite its name, was very basic. The wooden bench that served as a bed had a thin mat on top of it and a mosquito net around it. I was tired enough to drop off to sleep quickly but woke a couple of hours later, scratching. I could feel lumps where I had been bitten. After deciding I couldn't put up with it any longer, I used my torch to investigate. The first thing I saw was a rat scratching around in the corner of the room, but that wasn't my concern. Far more disturbing was the sight of bed bugs everywhere – on me, the blanket and the mat, and all over the mosquito net. I started a massacre – at least they weren't difficult to kill, like fleas. But I had hardly gone back to sleep before I felt more biting. I got up and went through all my bedding with my torch, determined not to miss a single one.

There was another shock the following morning when I found the river flooded. Samuel said that hundreds of logs had been swept away in the night. Andrew had to steer carefully to avoid them. At the Rivers Estate, Ray Kelly persuaded us to stay the night to avoid sailing in the dark and offered me a bed and clean sheets. Thinking I would save their linen I unpacked my own, but when I saw a bug on my pyjamas, I hastily tied my bundle up again!

One morning as I sat at the radio to contact Sandakan, I heard a familiar voice.

'Good morning, Wendy! Or should I say, "How are yer gannin', pet?"'

'Frank! You're back! How are you and Irene? How was Newcastle?'

He brought greetings from home, and gave me the news that Patrick was doing well. It was wonderful to hear him again.

'I'll give you more news when I see you at Easter, Wendy, but before you go, I have a telegram for you that Sister Christina has asked me to read to you. "Shall be in Kuching August. Please stay if possible. Lawrence."'

I had told Lawrence I would be visiting Kuching with my mother at the end of her holiday. It sounded as if he was inviting us to stay with him, but I had already arranged for us to stay with Anthony Perry, the provost of the cathedral there, which felt more appropriate. All the same, I was looking forward to seeing Lawrence again, and resolved to write back to him soon to give him our itinerary.

Easter – on 2 April – was early in 1961 so it didn't feel like five minutes before we were back in Sandakan, where we saw the Lomax family again. I thought that Frank and Irene both looked plumper after several months on a Western diet. Frank told me that an anonymous benefactor had left Joan and me a credit note for $35 each to spend in a local store.

'The requirement is that you spend it on yourselves, not the mission,' he stipulated.

On our return to Tongud, *Malaikat* was so loaded with barang that there was no room for us in the cabin. On a typical journey, as well as our personal belongings (including this time my new tape recorder) we might be transporting food and drink; supplies for the school, mission and dispensary; donated items from the government, Red Cross or Unicef; engine parts and agricultural equipment. This time I also had a present for Samuel: with some money sent from friends in Newcastle I had bought him a uniform consisting of three pairs of navy shorts, three white shirts and six handkerchiefs. I was hoping he might set an example to the patients by using the handkerchiefs rather than the dispensary floor when he needed to spit! I had recently placed large lidded enamel pots containing disinfectant at strategic points in and around the dispensary, and a few people were beginning to use them.

Joan and I sat on the sun-scorched deck, squeezing into whatever spot of shade we could find. After Balad we came across a launch that was stuck in the shallow water. Fearing that the same fate might befall us, Majang dropped anchor and tied us to a tree. All we could do was wait. Joan and I had fun deciding what three things or people we would choose to be stranded with on a desert island. We were hot and listless. We lay and listened to our transistor radio. The main news was of a Russian major who had been hailed a hero on becoming the first man in space, but there were few details so I was left with more questions than answers. We kept having to get up to chase away rats that were climbing the rope and coming on board to eat our food, but it was almost too much effort to move.

When I woke that night back in Tongud to hear a thumping sound close by, I thought initially that I was still on the boat. Remembering where I was, I feared we had an intruder. My torch wasn't to hand, so I lay in a cold sweat, listening and waiting. After what felt like ages, I dozed off again.

'A baby rat fell down from the roof,' Joan told me the next morning. 'A few seconds later a snake shot after it. I think it might be the one I saw by the jamban the other day. I'm worried now that it lives here, in the walls.'

'You should have shouted, Joan.'

'Well, it went under the cupboard after that and I couldn't really do anything.'

We searched in vain with thick sticks and my parang, but there was no sign of it. Our only hope was that it had left the house.

It was Tamu again, the festival that had marked my arrival the year before, and, as usual, everyone converged on Tongud. David Fielding, a newly appointed DO in the interior, and the forestry officer, John Burder, were among the colonial visitors, and both men were delighted when I was able to serve them iced beer in the dispensary, thanks to my fridge – and a funnel that fitted at last! A little later Frank arrived with Ray Kelly. Frank brought our post, which included two tapes for me from home. I was desperate to listen to them on my new tape recorder – that was proving to be a hit with all the locals, especially the schoolchildren, who loved to hear themselves – but with guests to feed and patients to see, it was hard to find a free moment.

This Tamu there were no government medical staff or even dressers (surgical assistants who ran some of the smaller dispensaries), and no extra medicines had been sent. I had recently unpacked a box of new equipment that had arrived from Unicef, but it was of little use without more pairs of hands. Seeing me struggle, Frank and John Burder stepped in to help Samuel and me one morning. Both were horrified to see a three-year-old child with huge abscesses all over her scalp. Frank held the child as I incised and drained the abscesses, and Mr Burder prepared the swabs, once he had recovered from his squeamishness.

I had been helping the children prepare a sketch that was part of a show for Tamu. Many of the visiting communities were also performing in the show. Our sketch was set in an operating theatre in which a patient with acute appendicitis, who had not responded to medical witchcraft, was now having his appendix removed by a doctor. The boys were having a last-minute rehearsal in the dispensary when Mr Fielding walked in on us and saw Stephen wielding forceps and scalpel over a fellow pupil, as I issued instructions. He turned white and had to be reassured that he was witnessing a play and that I was not teaching schoolboys to be surgeons!

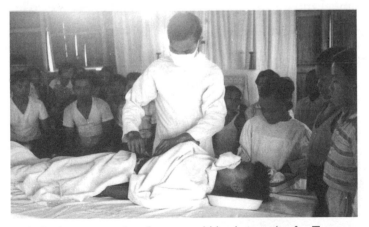

Imitation game: schoolboys copy Wendy in a play for Tamu

That night the concert was packed and the room was very hot. As more people arrived they hung on the beams or pushed in front of others so that they could get inside. I sat about halfway back with Mr Fielding, Mr Burder, Ray and Frank. The show was about an hour late starting, which added to our discomfort.

'Why the delay?' asked Frank. 'You might have more patients than you bargained for, Wendy, if we have to sit in this heat any longer.'

We found that we were waiting for the crew from Radio Sabah who had come to record the concert and conduct some interviews.

I watched our sketch, which got plenty of laughs.

'They say that imitation is a form of flattery,' whispered Ray Kelly, before I sneaked out to visit the child with the abscesses. She was sleeping, so I left medicine in case she woke up.

The next morning I saw 60 patients, and there was only Samuel and me to attend to them. How relieved I was to have

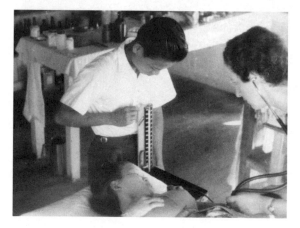

Samuel assists Wendy with a patient in the dispensary

my assistant! Samuel was kept busy sterilizing instruments, purifying water and fetching whatever I needed, as well as acting as interpreter. Later there was a *makan* (meal) in the courthouse, with chief Nyad and all the headmen and special visitors. Afterwards, Mr Fielding helped me to distribute boxes of salt and milk from the Red Cross and Unicef for the OTs to take back to their kampongs.

Everyone let their hair down on the last night of Tamu. I refused the tapai jar but found myself doing Malay-style dancing. It was nearly midnight when I excused myself. I was determined to record a tape to send back with Frank the next day. We had guests in our house, so the dispensary was the only place quiet enough. I had just sat down in the store room when John Burder came in to go to bed, so I moved to the kitchen. It took a while to think about what I wanted to say, but eventually I was satisfied and it was recorded. I dashed off two letters – to my parents and Sister Christina – and at 4.30 a.m. went to bed, not looking forward to rising an hour and a half later.

10

The first ice

May to June 1961

Samuel brought Larnia to the clinic, saying she had been having pains all day. I discovered she was having fairly strong contractions. I performed a pelvic examination and found the head mid cavity, the membranes intact. I gave her pethidine and prepared things for delivery. Just before dark, Samuel's parents arrived to join them in the dispensary for the night, but I told Samuel they should go home as it would be too many people. Samuel's mother wanted Larnia to have kampong medicine on her abdomen, but Samuel had been firm and told her that Christians didn't do such things.

I was pleased to see that Samuel was attentive to his wife, just as he was to the patients. They settled down on two camp beds. I went home and slept badly, half-expecting Samuel to come for me in the night. The next day Larnia's contractions were not so strong or as regular. She stayed in the dispensary while Samuel, in quieter moments, helped me with a garden I was planting between the dispensary and our house. I had wanted a garden of my own here ever since I had first seen Mrs Meyer's tropical garden in Sandakan. Here in the clearing, with abundant heat and water, I hoped it would flourish.

When school lessons were over, Samuel took some of the boys back to his house to help him dig up cannas and replant them in a trench he had dug. The brown, muddy ground was transformed into a plot of explosive colour.

When I checked in on him and Larnia that evening I discovered to my amusement that the novelty of the camp beds had worn off and they were both sleeping on the floor!

Joan and I listened to 'Here and there in North Borneo' on Radio Sabah. Ray Kelly was being interviewed about the Tongud Tamu, and spoke about our mission work.

'A British nurse and an Australian teacher live in a wooden house in a clearing on the Kinabatangan River,' said the introduction to the interview.

'It sounds like the start of a fairy tale!' said Joan, as we chuckled over the opening, and the sombre tones of the presenter. 'I wonder what happens to them next.'

We listened to Ray talk animatedly about how we had given up the comforts of our Western lives to answer a call from the Dusun people.

'Wow, do we know these girls?' I asked, as he sang our praises. By now we were feeling rather embarrassed.

I had just settled down to sleep when Joan called out that there was a snake in her room.

I suggested fetching Arnold or Andrew, but Joan said their lights were out so instead I grabbed my parang. Andrew and the boys had made an inner wall of kajang for our house – fresh pliable palm woven to make a flat material. While this hid the layer of bark and made the rooms more attractive than before, it had the disadvantage of providing more hiding spaces for unwanted visitors.

I could see the snake moving along the top of the wall above the window, between the two layers. It was about five feet long and four inches in circumference, and was black with shades of grey. It kept rearing its head up and flicking out its tongue. I put a chair on top of Joan's desk and stood on it, parang poised. I wanted to strike near the head but couldn't get close enough. Its tail end was more accessible, but I worried that it might lash out at me in fury, and neither Joan nor I had any idea how poisonous it was.

I considered going for Samuel, but when the snake disappeared within the wall there seemed little point.

'It probably lives there to feed on the rats,' I said, shrugging. 'Perhaps it's the lesser of two evils.'

We could hear it still, hissing like a cat.

'Wait till the listeners hear the next instalment,' said Joan. In the voice of the presenter, she went on, 'The two women share their bedrooms with rats and snakes, battling it out every night before bed with their parangs!'

'If they only knew the half of it! I'll get us both a sleeping tablet – I think we'll need one tonight.'

The next morning I taught Larnia, Samuel and his mother about labour and childbirth with the aid of a flannelgraph entitled 'Birth of a baby'. All three stared at it, fascinated, as if the whole process was a revelation to them. Samuel told me that in the kampongs the husband and two men pushed hard on the fundus during labour while a woman pulled at the other end, then one man pushed to expel the placenta. They would cut the cord with bamboo and bury the placenta in bamboo. I remembered my experience with childbirth when I had been with Beryl in Sarawak, not long after my arrival in Borneo, and how strange it had all seemed.

I was fairly certain my sleep was not going to be disturbed by a new baby that night, so after writing my diary and letters I played the *Messiah* and sat following the score, with Jeremy asleep on my lap. I couldn't resist joining in. Music and singing had always been a big part of my life. I could barely remember a time when I hadn't belonged to a choir. But it was now more than nine months since my tonsillectomy, and I still sounded husky and struggled to reach the high notes. What had happened to that clear voice that people used to compare to a choirboy's? Perhaps it was nothing to do with the tonsillectomy and was simply the effect of living in this unnaturally humid atmosphere. Or perhaps it was, and I just had to give it more time. I gave up and listened to 'Concert Hour' on Radio Sarawak.

At Mass the next morning, Arnold said special prayers for 'Mrs Elsie Grey, leaving England today to travel to Borneo; may God guide and protect her.' I felt so excited at the thought of Mum beginning her journey, and kept wondering what time she would be sailing and where she might be.

Before opening the dispensary I nipped to the jamban. As I was about to sit down I spotted a large snake in the hole. Was it the one from Joan's room? It looked rather like it. But wherever it had come from, I didn't want it making itself at home in our loo. I poured some kerosene into the hole and watched it wriggle. When I went back I couldn't see it, but I was still afraid to sit down. It was one thing having a snake on the wall in front of me, but quite another having it lurking below the most intimate part of my anatomy. I called for Samuel, who tried to fish it out but couldn't find it. We decided it must have died.

For some time now I had been concerned about our fellow mission worker Andrew, on whom we relied so much for his teaching, building and carpentry skills. He would be fine one moment, then at other times he seemed lethargic and depressed. At one point he stopped eating. Frank had been talking about sending him to help at a new mission at a place called Sapi but, after talking to Andrew, I had advised against another remote placement. Now his health had continued to deteriorate. It was clear to me that he needed to leave the interior and receive proper treatment in hospital. Arnold, Joan and I held an impromptu meeting at which it was decided that I should accompany Andrew to Sandakan, setting off the next day, and that we should ask Frank to book his passage to Kuching to see a specialist. I only hoped Larnia wouldn't deliver while I was away.

As mission nurse, I had been given the job of explaining this to Andrew. He sat silently at first, before expressing his unhappiness at the prospect. It took me some time to convince him that it was necessary. Arnold backed me up, and Andrew seemed to accept it in the end.

As we walked down to the river where *Malaikat Raphael* was waiting, we passed the site of the new chapel, where Arnold and Andrew were building a boat for the mission. Joan and I often joked that it looked more like a shipbuilding yard than a future place of worship!

'I will finish the boat when I return,' said Andrew, smiling at me. I had to fight back tears, for I knew he was unlikely to come back to Tongud.

Simon, one of the older boys, who had been learning the ropes from Majang, was our skipper, and we also took another pupil, David. It was David's first trip to Sandakan and as we got closer to the coast, his eyes grew wider. He could hardly believe the size of the ships in the port, and later, the sight of the cars and the buses on the roads.

I felt desperately sad as I watched Andrew board the plane to Kuching. I thought of all he had done for the mission – his cheerful enthusiasm, his practical talents and his love and care for the pupils. We were going to miss him hugely. I hoped and prayed he would get better quickly.

I was relieved to find that Larnia had still not had her baby when we returned. It was going to be a busy time for me, baby or no baby, as Arnold was going travelling for two weeks among the Ramanau and Menokok tribes and I was to stay behind and help with the school.

It was a pleasant change of routine for me. I woke to the sound of the pupils' bell at 5.45 a.m. After a couple of hours in the dispensary I went to teach English and poetry to the first and second years. I found them keen to learn and well behaved. Joan had made storybooks for the pupils, translating simple sentences from Dusun into English. One of them told of two boys who, while exploring in their canoe one day, saw a durian tree, which they climbed to pick the fruit. As the boys read to me, 'The durian is good,' I shook my head and pulled a face, causing them to giggle and to repeat the sentence louder. We did this several times until I had to calm them down. I had come to the opinion that the durian fruit was a taste only the locals could appreciate.

Before lunch Joan and I got the whole school together to teach them the Dashing White Sergeant. It did occur to me as I rested in my room later that only the British would be teaching Scottish country dancing in the tropics during the hottest part of the day!

We heard over the radio from Frank that Andrew was living at the House of the Epiphany in Kuching, where Anthony, the provost of the cathedral, was keeping an eye on him. Andrew was attending the hospital as an outpatient.

Eighteen-year-old Rasina brought her three-week-old infant, Linchur, to the dispensary. I feared it might be too late for him and, knowing the local superstitions, was afraid of him dying and frightening others away. However, I realized I must have faith and that he deserved all the care I could give him, just like anyone else. Moreover, as Rasina's late mother had been the witch doctor in Tongud, I felt that I had been honoured to be asked to help her child.

Linchur weighed 4 pounds 11 ounces and was extremely emaciated. He was gasping and crying all the time, and his breathing was very rapid and shallow. He had been ill for three days, said his mother, and there had been two mameows for him, with no result. It appeared to be pneumonia. I began his treatment that evening, after which he slept until 3.30 a.m. I stayed with them in the dispensary, on a camp bed beside the fridge. There had never been so many people sleeping in the dispensary as there were that night, with Samuel and Larnia in one room, and Rasina, her baby and small son Tering, her sister and her brother (who also wanted to stay) in another. I lay awake for hours waiting for the infant to cry. When he did, he fought against the bottle but was responsive to spoon feeding.

I left Samuel in charge the next morning while I went to teach. Another night in the dispensary followed. The baby cried and took three-quarters of an hour to soothe, before sleeping all the way through till morning. Rasina bathed him for the first time and prepared and gave him feeds, and he grew more settled.

I managed to return to my own bed that night, and Joan brought me breakfast the next day.

'Oh, what would I do without you!' I exclaimed.

'You can't keep burning the candle at both ends,' she said, sitting on the end of my bed. 'You're going to be a wreck by the time your mother arrives.'

'Yes, nurse!' I teased her. Then I added, 'Don't worry, Joan. It's the thought of her visit that's keeping me going. I heard from Sister Christina yesterday that she's in Port Said. When I looked at the Southern Cross last night I realized that it won't be long before she's looking at the same stars as we are.'

'Well, don't overdo it. If you find there's too much to cope with you might just have to tell Arnold and Frank and let them sort it out. We're not superhuman.'

It probably wasn't a miracle, but in the dispensary I found that the baby had slept well, and I arranged for him and his mother to go home after his next feed. I gave Rasina 12 rag squares to use as nappies, Lactogen and Glucodin, and lent her a feeding bottle and teat.

Two days after Rasina and her family left, I admitted another very sick baby. Sawal was about a year old and an orphan. He was being cared for by his aunt, the wife of a man called Uloh. He was very pale and emaciated, had gastroenteritis and an enlarged spleen, and was gasping for breath. I began his treatment then went to teach for an hour. When I came back I found hookworm in his stools. I slept in the dispensary again so that I could attend to him in the night, getting up constantly to give him chloral hydrate and glucose water. I didn't sleep much. I heard the boys start their manual work early, and at about the same time a dog started an awful din. There was no point in staying in bed any longer.

Sawal was still struggling to breathe, gasping and groaning. His abdomen was distended with flatulence, his muscles rigid.

'You poor child,' I thought. 'I wish I could do more to help you.'

A little later that morning Sawal went into spasm, collapsed and died. It was hardly a surprise, and yet I couldn't believe it – I refused to believe it. I tried in vain to hear the apex beat. Nothing. I looked at that tiny chest, sure that it would show a flickering movement at any moment. I had to save him. It was my job. My patients didn't die! And besides, as a nurse it was not my job to pronounce a death – that was what doctors did. By that strange logic, I convinced myself that Sawal was going to survive.

Eventually I had to accept the fact that he was gone. I felt huge sadness. I had done my best but it had been too late. I asked Samuel to break the news to Uloh's wife.

Without Arnold to advise me, I chose a spot for the grave down the bank beyond the site of the future church, and Uloh and some men dug a hole. It was a job to find a suitable box for a coffin, but eventually Joan came across a tool box in Andrew's room which was the perfect size. Andrew had made it, and we felt sure he would be happy about its new use. It was promptly washed out and dried in the sun. I bathed the baby and dressed him in a white cotton gown that had been sent by a friend from home – an antique, by the look of it, and beautifully embroidered. After lining the box with a sheet, I placed Sawal's tiny body inside, folded his hands, fingers interlocking, and placed a red hibiscus flower in them. By now a group of schoolchildren had appeared so we all knelt around the baby and I led simple prayers. Then the box was nailed up and carried out.

With Samuel leading the way and carrying the cross he had just made, on which he had carved the baby's name and the date, we processed to the site of the grave. There must have been about 25 of us, all singing 'Firmly I believe and truly' in Dusun. As the coffin was being buried we sang 'Holy, Holy, Holy' in Dusun, then I said another prayer, which Samuel translated, phrase by phrase, before we all processed back to the dispensary, still singing.

Uloh's wife, who had been in a terrible state, had stopped crying at the grave. She and her husband joined Samuel and me for iced orange squash in the dispensary kitchen. They were astonished at the sight of the ice, and kept touching it and laughing. I told them about snow and cold weather in England, and fetched some more ice from the fridge, thrusting it into their hands and making them squeal by rubbing it on their faces. I showed them some of my Christmas cards with their snowy scenes. It seemed to take their minds off the sad occasion.

I learned from them that Sawal's mother had died of a postpartum haemorrhage three or four days after her son's birth.

It was 3 p.m. and I still hadn't eaten lunch. Another sick child had been brought in that morning by his parents, who had their two other young children with them. I had seen eight-year-old Farouk a few weeks earlier and had wanted to admit him then, but his parents had taken him home, promising to bring him back if he didn't improve. The child was a pathetic sight. He could hardly walk, had an enormous abdomen and very thin limbs, and appeared to be suffering from an umbilical abscess and malnutrition. After the sad events of earlier in the day, his parents decided they would take him to the tamu house instead of staying in the dispensary. I urged them to reconsider so that I could observe and nurse the child, but they said they were afraid to stay.

They must have changed their minds, or someone must have spoken to them, for to my relief they returned at night-time, though they insisted on sleeping in the kitchen and refused to enter the room where the baby had died. After some effort I persuaded them to move into the room where the fridge was. I gave them toys for the other children and hot glucose water in a thermos for Farouk, then went home to mark some maths books. When I finally put them aside and went to bed I said a special prayer for Sawal, whose short life seemed to have been full of sorrow from the start.

I was going to Sandakan to meet Mum in a few days. Her arrival couldn't come soon enough for me now.

I thought Farouk looked better the next morning. But when I returned half an hour later, I found his mother feeding him rice and tinned fish. He sat there, his mouth covered in food and a puddle of vomit beside him. I learned that his father had gone home to bring the padi in and left his wife with the children. I told her if she was not prepared to cooperate, the treatment would be useless and there would be no point in her staying. She refused to stop feeding him and decided to take the child away.

After they had left I discovered they had used all of Samuel's sugar and had taken some toys and clothing belonging to the dispensary, so I sent Samuel to bring them back.

Samuel returned with the missing items, saying that Farouk's mother had told him they had heard knocking and strange sounds in the night.

'It was the baby, back from the grave,' he solemnly informed me. He asked if I would sleep in the dispensary that night with him and Larnia.

'Samuel, you know there is nothing to fear,' I said.

I was surprised and, I suppose, disappointed, too. Samuel, who had assured so many people that to believe in Christ was to reject traditional beliefs, was succumbing to those superstitions himself. All the same, I knew it was best to agree to his request.

I cheered up when Rasina came by to show me how well the baby was doing, and with a present of 16 eggs, to thank me for helping her, which I said I would share with Samuel.

That night I moved my camp bed into the dispensary and waited for Samuel and Larnia. They had only just arrived when Samuel said they could hear noises and there was a smell of something bad, inferring that it was linked with the death. I tried to dispel their fears through distraction. I gave Samuel the radio to play with – he was fascinated by radio sets and could happily spend ages twiddling the knobs to find different stations, seemingly unbothered by the interference that was sometimes the only result. I gave Larnia a bundle of *Life* magazines. I noticed how engrossed she was in them,

Rasina and her son, Tering

and when I glanced over her shoulder a little later, I couldn't help smiling when I saw that she was looking at them upside down.

At about 9 p.m. we settled down, though I was aware of every sound and of the effect it might be having on my companions. The fridge hummed, the trees and grasses rustled, and animal cries were carried in the air, sounding closer than they were. I was just drifting off when I heard the cat outside, scratching loudly against some wood.

'It's coming!' Samuel called to me, in terror.

I told him it was Jeremy and he went outside to make sure.

At about midnight a dog started howling. I got up and chased it away. It came back soon after and Samuel went outside and threw something at it. Finally we all settled down to a light sleep.

Farouk and his mother arrived the next morning. The child was still vomiting, but she still refused to cooperate over food, and they all trooped off again.

I felt exasperated. The child was more seriously ill than his mother realized. Perhaps if Arnold had been around he could have spoken to her, made her see sense.

Samuel and Larnia decided to go home that night, and Joan had gone to meet up with Arnold in Penungah. As I went to bed it dawned on me that this was the first time I had slept in the house alone. Furthermore, with no inpatients in the dispensary and no Andrew or Arnold next door, I had no near neighbours.

'Wendy Grey, you're as bad as they are,' I chastised myself, as I looked into the blackness outside with a small shudder. 'Have some faith. Time to practise what you preach.'

I slept well that night for the first time in ages.

I was worried about Farouk. I sent a message urging his father, Muhammad, to bring his son to the dispensary so that they could come to Sandakan with me when I went to meet Mum, but he replied that a mameow was about to begin and he would have to wait until it was over. Samuel went to speak to him and returned with Muhammad but no child. Muhammad explained that the mameow had started and the women had refused to let the child leave. He also said that if he were to go, the family would have nothing to eat. After another long discussion I loaned him some rice to take home, and he said he would bring Farouk back with him the next morning, but was adamant that the child would only stay in Sandakan as long as I was there, and that there was no question of a prolonged stay in hospital.

Joan and Arnold returned. Their boat had overturned and they had all ended up in the water, losing some of their barang, including some of Arnold's newly translated work, which was a big blow.

It was Sunday the next day and Farouk and his parents were at Mass. I thought the child looked worse, not helped by the white marks painted on him from the mameow.

We set off later that morning in *Malaikat Raphael*. The child vomited for much of the journey. One of the camps we had stayed in previously was now deserted, and we carried on to another where we were given a good meal of peacock and a bed for the night. The boys took several wrong turnings in the Trusan, and we were held up by log rafts, but the sea was calm. At the wharf in Sandakan I telephoned for an ambulance, which came quickly, and accompanied Farouk and his father to the hospital.

Back at the boarding house there were letters waiting for me from Mum, written from various ports. I rushed to the post office just five minutes before it closed to send her a telegram in Singapore: 'In Sandakan, longing Thursday, good flight.'

11

Travels with my mother

June to September 1961

I was walking along a steamy road in Sandakan with my
mother beside me. I kept looking at her, just to make sure.
She was more tanned than I was used to seeing her, but still
dressed like an Englishwoman, albeit with a few concessions
to the heat. After collecting her from the airport and
introducing her to everyone in the boarding house, I had
left her to sleep, then brought her breakfast in bed the next
day. Now we were off to the dressmaker to buy her some
sarongs, before a visit to the new air-conditioned café for an
iced drink.

'I can't believe you're really here!' I kept saying to her. 'Tell
me about everyone at home – Daddy, and Rhoda, and . . .'

'I think you're as up to date as I am, Wendy,' she said,
laughing. 'Don't forget I've been on a boat for the past month.'

The next day I left her at the opening of the new Red
Cross building by the Governor's wife, Lady Goode, while
Sister Christina took me to visit Farouk. He was very sick; his
doctor wanted him to stay in hospital for at least a month but
his father was still talking about them returning to Tongud
with me. Feeling rather tense from the effort of trying to keep
my patience with Muhammad, I went to the TB hospital to
see Simin, who gave me a lovely welcome. She was still thin,
but getting stronger.

There was a Red Cross dance that night and the Goodes
were special guests. Mum and I went along with Frank and

Irene, Jean and Barbara, and I introduced Mum to more people than she could possibly remember. We both danced with Frank, and were summoned, one at a time, to speak to Lady Goode.

'This is one side of my life here, Mum,' I said, as I looked at everyone in their finery. We might almost have been in Newcastle, or London. 'I suppose life in Sandakan helps me to keep going when the other part gets too much.'

Mum said that made perfect sense.

Just before we turned in for the night, Mum calmly extricated herself from her mosquito net to trap a moth and release it outside.

'Mum, you are truly unflappable,' I told her.

It seemed I could deal with rats and snakes when I had to, but I drew the line at moths, particularly ones that were the size of a man's outstretched hand when they flew.

'We get them in Healey all the time,' she said, not seeming to notice that this one was a Goliath compared to the moths of Northumberland!

We were in luck for the journey back to Tongud: the river was just right at every stage, with no rapids to negotiate and no logs to dodge. As we approached I could see Arnold and the boys and girls waiting to meet us on the bank, which Mum said made her feel like a royal visitor.

Remembering my own shock on arrival, I hoped I had prepared her for her new abode. Lily had kept the house clean and tidy. Mum had a good look round. Perhaps she was being kind, but she said she liked its 'rustic decoration'.

We were in bed early that night. Jeremy, who had been delighted to see us, was lying across my legs. I was in a deep sleep when I became aware that someone was saying my name. I found that Samuel was calling me from outside, telling me that he had brought Larnia to the dispensary as she was about to have her baby.

I pulled on some clothes and dashed across. This time she was having fairly strong contractions. I gave her pethidine and asked Samuel to call me if the pain got worse or if there was any sign of the baby's head. Samuel's mother and father had come too, and were making themselves at home. I went back to bed and dozed off again. Shortly after six I was about to get up to go and check on Larnia when there was a knocking on the wall. It was Samuel's mother to tell me that the baby had been born.

In the dispensary I found only the grandmother, Larnia and the baby – a boy – present. Samuel had gone home to fetch a cooking pot. I cut the cord then expelled the placenta, bathed the baby and dressed him, and placed him in the improvised cot, before bathing Larnia. I was delighted that he appeared to be a healthy little chap, more robust than most of the newborns I had seen.

'Talk about timing it well,' I said to Mum as I showed her round the dispensary later that morning.

We asked the new parents what the baby was going to be called.

'Philip,' said Samuel proudly.

'One of the twelve apostles,' said Mum. 'A very nice name.' She looked at me and nodded her approval.

Samuel went to the radio I had bought for him in Sandakan and given him the previous afternoon. I had wondered if the gift might end up driving me mad, but had relented in the end. It didn't surprise me that he had grabbed it as he made his emergency journey to the dispensary in the early hours of the morning. He proudly rubbed his finger across the raised letters of the brand name.

'He is Philip, like the radio,' he told us, beaming.

'The nuns usually washed in there when they were with me,' I said to Mum.

I pointed to the drum on the little platform of what we euphemistically called our bathroom. The nuns would go inside it to bathe in private.

'I'm doing what you're doing,' said Mum. 'I wasn't a nun the last time I checked.'

Wearing our sarongs, we set off along the path to our bathing spot. Mum's sarong loosened as we walked and she refused to let me tighten it. It had practically fallen off her by the time she was in the river.

Wendy is accompanied by her mother, Elsie Grey, on a visit, and for her daily bath

'Stay under the water,' I instructed her, seeing how it was barely covering her. But she took little notice, and when she emerged she was revealing more than she was hiding.

'See how everyone's watching,' I chastised her, as I pointed to an audience that had appeared on the river bank, but she tutted and said that she didn't really think anyone was interested in looking at a 61-year-old Englishwoman.

'Aren't mothers surprising sometimes?' I said to Joan later. 'She would never behave like that in England, not even in our own back garden. She wears a hat and gloves whenever she goes out.'

The next time we went I fastened her sarong for her very tightly.

'Be decent, please,' I told her, but she just laughed at me.

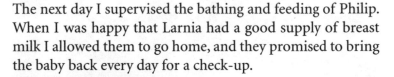

The next day I supervised the bathing and feeding of Philip. When I was happy that Larnia had a good supply of breast milk I allowed them to go home, and they promised to bring the baby back every day for a check-up.

Larnia and Samuel with their baby son, Philip

Mum took photos of the new family before they left. She was adapting well to life on the mission, and was never afraid to get her hands dirty, helping me in whatever way she could. She was fascinated by everything she saw, and her camera was usually in her hand.

Farouk's father had relented and allowed him to stay in hospital. However, worried about work and his harvest, he had returned himself. We heard from Sister Christina – who had gone to see the child and taken him fruit and crayons – that he was contented and making good progress, so Mum and I set off to the home of Muhammad to pass on the news to the family. He was in the forest getting rotan but we gave the message to his two wives. The house was full of naked children running around, and Mum asked if she could take some photos of them, whereupon they all disappeared and returned in their best clothes!

Having been nursing in Tongud for more than a year now, I had become accustomed to some of the sights that had shocked me in the early days. But there were inevitably still times when something caused me to take a deep breath before I could summon all of my professionalism and deal with it. I was keeping an eye on two pregnant women who were staying in the tamu house and reporting every day to the dispensary. On this particular day one of them brought her sister with her when she came for her check-up. The woman came shuffling towards me, her knees bent, her bottom just a few inches from the ground. She had been like this for three years, she said, unable to straighten her legs past the sitting position. I saw the scars of yaws on her face and body and realized that the crippling was almost certainly a result of the tertiary stage of the disease. Yet she was the most bright, cheerful soul imaginable and lifted the spirits of everyone around her. I would have done anything to wave a wand and cure her instantly. She said she would love to have her legs straightened, and that if it couldn't be done here in Tongud, well, she would be prepared to go to Sandakan. When I thought of the battles I fought to get people to go to hospital in the town!

I didn't know if they would be able to correct the deformity, but I promised to find out and let her know. After giving her penicillin, she went away, all smiles and thanks.

Dr Christiansen was now based in Jesselton, so as soon as I could I left a message for his replacement, Dr Cameron. I received an answer the next day that he would come to Tongud in August and see my patient himself. (I was away in August and, sadly, I don't know the outcome of that case – one of too many that I saw during my time in Borneo.)

It was mid July and the end of the school year. At the final Mass before the children went home to their kampongs, Arnold preached a special sermon. He told them what they must do (be kind to others, say their prayers) and not do (tell lies, steal, work on Sundays, take part in mameows). I looked at their keen, well-intentioned faces. They all loved and respected Arnold, and I knew they wanted to please him. But some of them were so young, I felt we could hardly expect them to stick to a code of behaviour that might not be practised within their families. In other ways, however, they were simply smaller versions of their parents: little men and women who hunted with blowpipes and parangs, cut down rotan and could look after themselves in ways that would

Work and play: children from the mission school, Tongud

severely test Western children. I looked at them as they nodded and smiled, eager to please 'Fadder', and I couldn't help smiling too.

Samuel took Mum and me on a trek – we wore shirts and shorts, socks and canvas shoes, and we soaped ourselves as protection from leeches. It was already hot when we left the house not long after breakfast and set off through the mission rubber terraces. Samuel was building a new house, which he proudly showed to Mum. It had a large zinc roof and the main part had a floor of flat planks he had cut from tree trunks. There were separate rooms for his parents, his nephew and himself, a kitchen, and plans for a bathroom. A large pendulum clock hung in the living quarters, though, didn't appear to work. His bedroom had one bark wall, a shelf for sleeping, a table and stools. And on the table stood the radio.

Larnia, wearing my old spotted seersucker dress, proudly showed us Philip, in a dress made out of SPG bale, and gave us a drink. In Samuel's old kampong, a 20-minute walk away, we saw his padi planted over the hillside, his tapioca and vegetables. We also visited the house of Abing, a 15-year-old Christian schoolboy who was to be married later that day. The wedding had only been arranged the day before.

As we were walking I heard a lovely singing voice. Samuel said it was Lily, and we caught sight of her working on the hill, and called out to her and waved. The sound was rather like yodelling, and was the way Dusuns sang when they were working.

We followed the path to a neighbouring kampong. Samuel cut a small tree trunk for Mum to use as a stick. It was an interesting walk for Mum, with logs to walk along and clamber over, and hills to cross. In some places Samuel had to use his parang to cut a way through. The path was slippery in parts and we both fell down a couple of times, but we were spared the leeches.

When we returned three hours later I was told that an incomplete radio message had arrived for someone called Captain Mills. None of us had heard of him, but he turned up the next day. Robert Mills was a British Army captain working for the survey department. He was doing some work in the area and I offered him a bed for the night in the dispensary, which was quieter now that the new parents had left. He ate with us and joined us that evening at the end-of-year party in the boys' boarding house. Gongs rang out, people danced, and Simon organized a game rather like forfeits. At the end the older boys – Simon, Ederiss and John, the brother of Helena – each made a speech in Malay, which Arnold translated. They thanked their parents, everyone in Tongud and all of us at the mission for what we had done for them. Ederiss, always one for words, added that it was as if the people of Tongud had been asleep, and now their eyes had been opened to the benefits of the mission.

'We are very happy to have Fadder, Sister and Miss Goodricke,' he said, looking at us all with such fondness I felt my eyes sting.

'You must be very proud of them all,' said Captain Mills to Arnold as we were leaving.

'I am,' said Arnold, adding, as he looked at Joan and me, 'We all are.'

Mum and I were leaving for Sandakan the next day. I boiled eggs for us and Captain Mills – our hens were keeping us well supplied – before he set off with his men to do some clearing in the forest.

There were 15 of us on *Malaikat Raphael*, including five boys whom we dropped off in their kampongs along the way, and Muhammad, who was going to bring Farouk home. Mum was fascinated by the grey monkeys in the trees, and Arnold pointed out to her a five-foot-long lizard on the bank. We spent the first night in Kuamut, arriving just before a storm began, and were offered a dirty house to sleep in. We ate rice and corned beef sitting on wooden boxes and kerosene tins. It was an uncomfortable night, lying on a hard floor with rats scuttling around and bats flying overhead. I saw Mum flinch a few times, but she had clearly made up her mind to take it all in her stride.

Back in Sandakan Frank lent me the new parish car and I went to see Farouk. Fatter and stronger, he was almost unrecognizable from the boy I had admitted a few weeks earlier, and pleased to see his father and to be going home.

I introduced Mum to my friends, Tony and Dorothy Meyer. Being green-fingered herself, Mum took great pleasure in Mrs Meyer's garden, and told her about the large vicarage gardens she and my father had tended over the years.

We made several trips to the beach known as Sandy Plain, often joined by the sisters, Jean and Barbara.

'Mum! I can't believe it! I don't think I've ever seen you swim properly, with no feet on the bottom,' I exclaimed when I saw her slicing her way through the water.

Mum laughed. 'It must be the first time I've swum in warm water. What a treat! I might stay in it all day.'

I laughed too. She looked delighted. I was pleased and proud that I was helping to give her a holiday to remember. If only Daddy could have come too, I thought, though

I always knew that was impossible when he had a parish to look after.

We sat under the shade of a tree and had squash, shortbread and petits fours made by Sister Christina.

'Mrs Grey, Wendy makes the most delicious lemonade from a recipe of yours. I wonder if you might make some while you're here,' said Jean, much to Mum's delight.

When we got back we went with Jean to the cheap matinee at The Cathay to see *Show Boat*. Later Mum and I sang together and played the school piano. One of my favourite Girl Guide songs was 'Land of the silver birch', a Canadian folk song, and we talked about my brother Joe, who was living in the wilds of Saskatchewan as a teacher in a tiny school. In some ways he was as isolated as I was, travelling by horseback every Sunday night from the farm where he lived to put the heating on in the school for the start of the week. Joe and I had always been very close and he sent me thoughtful gifts for Christmas and birthdays. I must have been the only person in the interior of North Borneo with matching pink sheets and pillow cases on my bed!

'Do you mind that we're both so far away?' I asked Mum. I probably wouldn't have said it anywhere else, but it felt a safe question in this intimate moment.

Mum didn't even hesitate. 'All you want is for your children to be happy and fulfilled. I couldn't ask for anything else.'

After supper, Jean, Novice Prisca, Mum and I played Scrabble before Compline. It had been a special day, and I think Mum and I felt closer than we ever had.

We flew to Jesselton, where we were greeted by lots of old friends, including Bishop and Mrs Wong; Peggy Miles, the bishop's secretary; Flo Martin, principal of St Agnes' School; teacher Sheila Merryweather; and Father Briggs, who was back in the city after his spell standing in for Frank in Sandakan.

We were staying with Dr Christiansen, who showed us to a room with windows on three sides, giving us commanding views of the hills and the sea. A ceiling fan turned, and a gentle breeze fluttered the curtains. We even had our own bathroom with a bath we could stretch out in. Luxury indeed!

Later that day we were invited to a Rotary dinner where we met the Anglican priest, Father Burn, and his wife, Sybil. Alan Burn – newly arrived since my last visit – had been inspired to come to Borneo after hearing Frank speaking during his furlough, and had left his parish in Darlington to become Rector of All Saints', Jesselton. Bishop Wong told the guests that Mum and I had come from as far as England in distance and Tongud in travelling time!

I met Miss Waites again, the colony matron, who said she would like to see something of nursing in the interior, and we planned that she would visit me in Tongud. She took us to her flat in a huge government-built block which overlooked Likas Bay and the harbour, where over tea and scones she told us about her nursing experiences during the last war.

Mum told her, 'My husband was a dispatch rider during the First World War. He was a very young man then. He won't speak about his experiences, not even to Wendy or my son Joe.'

We had tours of the TB and general hospitals and met the sister of the maternity department, who had trained at Charing Cross.

'It's so lovely to see the medal again!' I exclaimed, looking at her uniform. 'And so far from home.'

'Charing Cross nurses do get around,' she said. 'There's at least one more of us here in Jesselton. Make sure you write to the League to let them know what you're doing!'

Arriving at Bishop Wong's new house for coffee one morning, Mum stopped in the driveway and nudged me. There stood a shiny black dustbin with 'Bishop Wong' painted in large white letters on the lid and the side.

'I feel as if he's going to jump out on us, rather like the magic act we saw last night,' she whispered. We were giggling like schoolgirls as we rang the doorbell, and had to quickly compose ourselves.

The magician had been Mr John Calvert, an American, who had hypnotized people so that their hands and feet seemed stuck to the floor; while blindfolded, he had been able to identify what members of the audience were holding. I had held up a stamp, confident that he could not have seen it nor been helped by anyone else. I was astounded when he correctly identified it.

On another day we were collected by Mr and Mrs McCartney and taken to their private box at the races. He was secretary of the Turf Club. It was the first time I'd been to the races, and Mrs McCartney showed me how to place a bet. I put a dollar on several horses and had a few small winnings, which I gave later to St Agnes' School.

'What would your father say?' said Mum, pretending to be shocked. But I could see she was enjoying herself as much as I was.

After two weeks in Jesselton we boarded the boat for our voyage to Kuching and the final stage of Mum's holiday. Father Briggs and Bishop Wong came to see us off. One of our fellow travellers was a priest called Father Tudball, who had been working in Beaufort in the interior and was going to take over a parish in Labuan, a group of islands. He seemed uncertain about his new mission and Mum, in particular, provided a sympathetic ear. We went on shore with him when we reached Labuan and set off to see his church and rectory, both of them filthy and neglected. There was no furniture in the rectory apart from a table and some upright wooden chairs, a couple of dirty-looking beds and a broken old Dover stove, caked in cooking stains. We accompanied Father Tudball to the shops, where we trailed around looking for furniture. We came back with four deckchairs, some buckets and a mat. He ordered food at cold storage and enquired about getting someone to help him scrub out the house.

'That poor man,' said Mum later, and he was in my thoughts too as we sailed again that night.

The next day we entered a wide river, fringed by nipa palms, and saw our destination in the distance. We anchored and everyone scrambled into a launch. Through my field glasses I saw someone in a long white cassock on the shore: Anthony Perry, our host. I had met Anthony on my first visit to Kuching, fresh off the boat from the UK. I had been instantly attracted to this tall, slim, good-looking man, the Provost of St Thomas's Cathedral, though I sensed the feeling was one-sided. Anthony greeted me like an old friend and welcomed Mum warmly. He drove us to his house where, to my delight, Andrew was waiting to see us before moving on somewhere new. I thought he looked well, and happier than I had ever seen him. I knew his departure from Tongud had been the right thing.

Anthony was a thoughtful and attentive host, who made sure that Mum and I saw something of the day-to-day life in

Kuching and some of the church and government projects that were taking place there, as well as taking us for swims and picnics. One day we drove to Padawan, where I had stayed soon after my arrival in Borneo, and saw some of the developments there, though, sadly, Gwynnedd was on leave.

On another day, Rob Anderson, the forestry officer, showed us their primary rainforest reserve, where each tree was numbered and labelled. He invited us to his home for tea later. We had to cross the river by sampan to his very old house, which he told us sometimes flooded.

One of the first people who came to call was Lawrence. We spent a lot of time with him when Anthony was working. He and Mum sat and listened as I read to them something I had written for an interview I had been asked to record on Radio Sarawak. I had spent ages preparing it, but their reactions weren't what I'd been hoping for.

'The trouble is, Wendy,' began Lawrence, trying not to hurt my feelings, 'you've grown so used to Tongud and your life there that you're making it all sound normal, run of the mill. Remember that your average citizen of Kuching – of most towns in Borneo, in fact – knows nothing about Tongud. It's as alien to him or her as it is to your friends back in Newcastle. So don't be afraid to go into more detail about exactly what it's like.'

Mum nodded her agreement. 'You should see her at work, Lawrence! It really is the middle of nowhere, and there she is, with none of the mod cons we've got back home. I don't know how she does it.'

And so I rewrote my speech, putting back some of the shock and surprise that I would have included without a second thought if I had been newly arrived in Tongud.

While Mum was having coffee with the ladies from church I went to see Lawrence about the North Borneo census figures. We had been talking and I was about to leave when he broke off what he was saying, took a step towards me and enfolded me in a passionate embrace. I succumbed for a couple of seconds, taken by surprise, then gently pushed him away.

'I must go, Lawrence. I'm sorry.'

My face felt hot as I marched back to Anthony's. Where had that come from? Had I let Lawrence think my feelings for him were anything other than platonic? Was it my fault? He had been so kind to me, and now to my mother as well, but was he looking for something deeper? I valued the friendship between us and didn't want to lose it, but feared that it might be over. Bother! Why did men have to spoil things? I remembered back in London in my days at Charing Cross when I had been taken to the cinema by a gynaecological consultant. During the film he took hold of my hand, then guided it to the most intimate part of his anatomy. I froze. I was 20 years old and had no idea men behaved liked this. I was older now, and a little more worldly wise, but this had still come out of the blue. I felt I still had a lot to learn about men!

'We heard you on the radio! Weren't you marvellous!' the ladies cried when I got back.

I managed to put on a bright face for them all, but my mind was elsewhere for most of that day.

Mum and I had arranged to meet Lawrence the next morning, and he and I both behaved as if nothing had happened. He took us to the open market for a Chinese makan, and that evening we went for a moonlight drive by the river. If only I was in love with him, I thought, how romantic this would be! I wondered what Mum would think if I were to tell her what had happened. Would she be surprised? Shocked? Well, I had no intention of saying anything.

When we managed to find a few minutes on our own, Lawrence apologized.

'We're both such a long way from home, Wendy, and, well, I never expected to meet a kindred spirit here. I'd rather hoped you felt the same way. We get along so well, don't you think? But I'm sorry if I shocked you. I hope we can stay friends.'

'Oh, Lawrence. Please don't apologize. I'm probably to blame too. I think very highly of you and I'm very sorry if I've ever given you the wrong idea. You've been the most wonderful friend to me here and I could never thank you enough.'

We had a quick, slightly awkward hug, but the air felt clearer.

Mum and I had been invited to tea by Lady Waddell, wife of the Governor of Sarawak, who had got in touch after hearing me on the radio. A taxi dropped us by the river where the Governor's sampan was waiting to take us to the other side. It was rather luxurious for a sampan, with comfortable cushions scattered around. Lady Waddell met us at the steps on the landing stage, looking very elegant in a lemon-coloured linen sheath dress and white shoes. Government House – also known as the Astana – had been built for the second rajah, Charles Brooke, former ruler of Sarawak. The thick red carpets felt like something from another world to one who had been living in such basic conditions for so long. We chatted over tea of egg sandwiches, drop scones and lemon drizzle cake. Lady Waddell was very natural, with no airs and graces. She showed us the library in an old tower, and the banquet room, where paintings of former rajahs lined the walls. After that we walked in the grounds and admired the orchids, before she saw us off in the sampan and stood waving for a few minutes.

'Talk about how the other half live!' Mum said to Lawrence that night.

He was accompanying me on Anthony's piano. He assured me that my voice was better than it had been the last time we had practised together.

'And she wore white shoes!' said Mum.

'So might you if you had someone to clean them for you,' I said.

'Tschh! Chance would be a fine thing.'

After we had finished our recital, Lawrence took us to the open market for prawns and beer.

'He is a very fine man,' said Mum later, after he had dropped us back at Anthony's.

'He certainly is,' I agreed.

On Mum's last day Anthony took us out for a picnic. We drove along a road that was dotted with rocks and potholes until we reached a river. It was very low, and we sat in the shade, our feet dangling in the cold clear water, while we ate our lunch. We drove further to a deeper part of the river where Anthony and I could swim, and I had just done a few strokes of breaststroke when I thought I saw a snake in the water.

'That's not a snake; that's a crocodile,' said Anthony, and we got out pretty quickly.

Anthony drove us to the airport. Lawrence came dashing in just as Mum was about to depart. He squeezed my shoulder and I knew he understood how I was feeling. I was happy he was there. We watched Mum climb the steps to the plane and she suddenly looked so vulnerable, I had to fight back my tears.

After we had said goodbye to Lawrence, Anthony took me to a market garden where we saw lots of New Guinea creeper, just like Dorothy Meyer had in her garden.

'I wish I could take this home,' I said. 'I would think of Borneo every day and all the people I've met here.' Then I added, 'Though I'm sure I'll think of them all anyway. Borneo isn't a place anyone could forget!'

12

An intruder

September to October 1961

It was a surprise to find a welcoming party in Jesselton, as I was only there to pick up Miss Waites and change planes. All the same, Father Briggs, Dr Christiansen, Flo, Peggy and Father Burns were all there. We had coffee and chatted before Miss Waites and I boarded our plane to Sandakan.

Frank and Sister Christina met us in Sandakan and took us to the boarding house, where Joan was waiting, desperate to catch up on all my news. She and I shared a downstairs room and let Miss Waites have the best one, the one I sometimes slept in.

Wendy and her patient Simin, before and after her treatment for TB

'I've been desperate for you and your thinning shears,' said Joan, whose hair was almost as thick as mine. 'And look, I've got this nasty boil on my arm.'

We hugged each other and laughed. It was good to be together again.

The next morning I went to see Simin in the TB hospital. I could hardly believe this was the young woman whose cadaverous body had shocked me on our first meeting.

'Simin, you look so pretty!' I told her.

It was true. Her cheeks were plump, and her arms and legs had filled out. She had lost that sad, haunted look I had seen on her face before.

She had been told she could go home soon, and I said I would collect her when I brought Miss Waites back to Sandakan in a couple of weeks' time.

There were four passengers on our return to Tongud. Siew Mann was a young Chinese woman who was training to be a teacher and would be helping Joan with the younger pupils for the rest of the term. We were grateful to have her, if only for a few months.

Malaikat's cabin, with its two bunks, was barely big enough for all our barang, so we had to take off some of the dried milk and clothing we had been given by the Red Cross. That would be brought on the next trip. The four of us sat in the hold, a canvas awning above us. The sea was calm.

Lawrence had given me a gift of a pair of binoculars when I had left Kuching. Looking through them, I saw a small boat coming towards us. It was the survey boat, and as it got closer I could see Captain Mills on board. We waved and shouted our greetings as we passed each other.

Later that afternoon there was a huge thunderstorm. We huddled into the tiny cabin, but rain poured through the gaps around the windows and soaked us and our belongings anyway. In the early evening, Majang moored beside a house and managed to cook rice for us all; it was quite a job, with the stove on the floor in the tiniest of spaces, and barely room to move. After eating we went to the house to ask if we could spend the night there, and the owners agreed. We climbed a notched pole to a bare room, where Joan, Siew Mann and I lay on the plank floor and Miss Waites on a camp bed.

We all had a bath the next morning using a bucket at the back of *Malaikat*. Miss Waites didn't seem bothered by the arrangement. She really was the easiest travelling companion.

Not long after we left I saw the strangest sight.

'I've just seen a monkey swimming,' I called to the others. 'Look quickly, over there!'

Joan squinted, shading her eyes from the sun. 'It's not April Fool's Day, is it?'

'Breast stroke or front crawl?' asked Miss Waites.

I laughed. 'I think it was more like doggy paddle.'

I'm not sure that the others believed me, and it was the first and only time I ever saw this.

We sailed for 16 hours until we reached Camp Pin, where, remembering the bed bugs, we chose to stay on the boat. There was only room for three to sleep in the hold so I squashed into the cabin on a bench that was too short for me while the others fixed one large mosquito net over themselves. It had been a long day and I fell asleep quickly, though I had taken a sleeping tablet to be sure.

I woke at 2.30 a.m. Something was touching me. Half doped, I put out a hand to discover what it was. To my horror I found I was touching a human hand, which had come through the window beside me and slipped underneath my net. The hand pulled away and I heard a scuffling and hurried footsteps. I sat up with a start, just in time to see a man dart into the cabin of the Chinese launch tied up alongside our boat. Not dreaming he would come back, I closed the window and tried to settle down – not easy when I was aware of my heart hammering violently in my ribcage. About ten minutes later I became aware of a light moving in my cabin and opened my eyes. A torch was shining through one of the other windows, and now it moved to illuminate my three companions, who were all sleeping soundly. The owner of the torch then came back to my window and began to open it. This time I felt sure my heart would leap out of my chest. I grabbed my own torch, shone it at the intruder and yelled at the top of my voice. He shot back on to his boat and into his cabin. The others had woken now and wanted to know what was happening.

Majang manoeuvred *Malaikat* away from the Chinese launch. I closed and locked all four cabin windows and the door. The cabin was like a furnace now, but better safe than sorry. Before lying down I took a look through the window. I could still see the man, standing on his boat, gazing over at ours. I shuddered. I doubted I would sleep again but managed to doze for a bit, and a couple of hours later I heard Majang starting the engine. The feeling of motion comforted me and I slept properly for a couple of hours.

We arrived at Lamag at noon. A pile of letters was waiting. Captain Mills was there too, talking to Mr Roberts, the Assistant District Officer (ADO).

'Ah, the jungle midwife and jungle teacher!' he said when he saw Joan and me. 'I've been telling people about both of you and the set-up you've got in Tongud. Most extraordinary.'

He asked if we had enjoyed our summer vacation, and we introduced him to Siew Mann and Miss Waites.

'You must call me Rob,' he said. 'I imagine we'll all be seeing a lot more of each other.'

The steering ring broke several times on the way back and Majang kept fixing it with cord, but when the engine stopped altogether he knew it was something serious. Fortunately we were within sight of a camp, whose workers towed us ashore. One of the engineers informed us that there were problems with the piston and we would need a new part, which would have to come from Singapore. We were stuck, though thankfully not too far from home. We stayed in the camp that night, and the next day Majang found a perhau to paddle Miss Waites and me upriver to Tangkulap, where some of the boys were waiting for us with *Malaikat Raphael*. Joan and Siew Mann would be picked up later.

Walking into our house was a depressing sight. It was thick with dirt, leaves and cobwebs.

'I'm so sorry,' I said to Miss Waites. 'This isn't much of a welcome for you.'

'There's no need to apologize, Wendy,' said Miss Waites. 'I can assure you that when you've been nursing for as long as I have, there are few things that truly bother you. Now, where are your cleaning materials?'

It was dark by the time we had finished working. Miss Waites declared that our home was perfectly charming. I remembered Mum saying something similar. I suspected, though, that what they were both thinking was something like, 'Are you sure this is your house and not the garden shed?!'

But something was missing.

'I haven't seen my cat,' I said anxiously. 'My assistant, Samuel, has been looking after him, but Jeremy usually appears when he hears me. And he likes meeting new people.'

'Is he happy living here?' asked Miss Waites.

'Well, he's been here most of his life. The dangerous animals tend to keep away from the settlement, though we have our share of snakes and scorpions.'

I called for him before going to bed but there was no sign of him. I hoped he was all right.

As we were having breakfast I could see people starting to arrive at the dispensary. I rushed my last mouthfuls, telling Miss Waites to take her time and join me when she was ready.

After attending to everyone I went to the OT's house, where his wife and two other people had malaria. I also popped in to see Rasina, and found that Tering, her older son, and the baby both had a fever. As some of the boarders had returned from their kampongs after the long vacation with high temperatures – I suspected some of them might have malaria, too – there was barely time for a break that day. I was more than ready for my bathe when I took Miss Waites to our spot in the river. It was very full, and all the shingle on the bank had been washed away.

'This has to be the best time of the day,' I said, adding hastily, 'not that I don't love everything else I do.'

Miss Waites laughed and said she understood perfectly.

The next day, after checking on the boarders, Miss Waites and I set off upriver for Penungah so that she could see one of the smaller dispensaries. Penungah did not have a doctor or a nurse but a dresser, who was trained to deal with minor wounds and illnesses. Chief Nyad greeted us when we arrived. The dresser, Joseph, opened the dispensary – a small atap building with an earth floor – and Miss Waites sat down and began to look at his books. I noticed that the poor fellow was shaking with fright as he stood there.

'She doesn't bite,' I said, patting his arm. In truth, I couldn't think of a less fearsome matron than Miss Waites, but he continued to look terrified.

Miss Waites asked to see the two village midwives. The first was about 45 years old, dressed in Western clothes and of clean appearance. On being questioned she told Miss Waites that she washed her hands with soap before every delivery, and cut the cord with bamboo. Miss Waites told her she mustn't use bamboo as babies could get tetanus from it. She asked her if she would like to do the one-month training course in Sandakan, and the midwife said she would like to very much. The other woman was a few years younger and also keen to train, but as she had three small children, this didn't seem possible for the time being.

We left Penungah at 2 p.m. and all was going well until we got stuck on some rocks going down a strong, deep rapid. Our paddler, Simon, and the boy with him disembarked and spent ages trying to push and pull us off, but the boat wouldn't budge. To try to help, I got out and climbed on to a big rock. It did the trick and the boys managed to free the boat. Now I had the problem of getting back into it. I clambered over the rocks towards it and stepped into the rushing water. I could feel the current, strong enough to knock me off my feet. My dress was hampering my progress so I picked up the skirt of it and tucked it into my collar, which amused Miss Waites very much.

'Safety before modesty,' I said.

'I think it's a very wise motto,' she replied.

It was a huge help having someone with the experience of Miss Waites around for a few days. Despite her seniority and experience, she was a sweet, humble lady and, rather like my mother, seemed game for anything. On a quiet afternoon, Samuel and David took us in a perhau up the River Tongud, which was very high, muddy and flowing fast.

'It's exciting when it's like this,' I told her, grinning, 'although not as pretty. Mind you hold on tight here!'

I had grown used to travelling in dugout canoes, but it was important to remain still as they were easily overturned. Once, during an overnight stay on a timber camp, when I had been invited to join a party on a hunting expedition, I had made the mistake of standing up to stretch my stiff legs and had fallen headfirst into the river. My main concern was that I had tipped our prey – a huge wild pig – overboard, but my crew, who anxiously hauled me back on board, told me there were crocodiles nearby and I was very lucky they hadn't come to investigate.

'I can see that you can cope with anything, Wendy,' Miss Waites said, taking me by surprise. 'The trickier things are, the more you step up to the occasion.'

I was flattered, but I felt it didn't tell the whole story.

'There are times when I feel woefully unprepared for what I have to do here,' I admitted. 'I suppose things have been quite straightforward while you've been here, but sometimes when I'm looking through *Gray's Anatomy* I'm only too aware how badly things could go wrong.'

Her visit was over all too soon. On our return to Sandakan, Miss Waites said that her stay in Tongud had really opened her eyes to the way of life in the interior.

'I've been thinking about what you said to me about feeling ill-prepared, and thought you might come to Jesselton for a month later in the year. You would be my guest, and spend time with the doctors in the hospitals and clinics. You could watch what's going on and ask all the questions you want.'

I said it sounded like a great idea. Frank agreed, but suggested waiting until the new year.

I travelled back to Tongud with Simin. The sea was too rough for *Malaikat Raphael* and Mr Hunt arranged for a bigger boat to tow us over the bay before we transferred back into the jungkung.

I caught up on my letters as we sailed. I wrote to Miss Waites, and to the other nurse I respected so much: Miss Stephenson. I couldn't help thinking that Miss Stephenson, who had worked in refugee camps during the war, and in Borneo had reputedly delivered the baby of a headhunter, would get on splendidly with Miss Waites.

On the river bank we stopped to look at a nine-foot-long crocodile which had just been caught using the skin of a deer as bait. The crocodile was attached to a large hook tied to a length of rotan, and was still moving. It had a pungent smell. Though these dark-green and black creatures normally sent a shiver down my spine, I felt sorry for this one. The men who had caught it told us that they didn't eat the flesh but expected to get $50 for the skin.

Back in Tongud, Simin slept in the dispensary that night. I took photos of her, and showed her some I had taken before she was admitted. She gasped at the sight of herself and put her hand to her throat. I told her that with her permission I would like to use a before and after photo to help persuade other TB sufferers to go to Sandakan for treatment like she had done. When she agreed, I pinned these up in the small waiting area of the dispensary where I knew they would be noticed and commented on.

Jeremy reappeared. I was shocked to see how thin and mangey he was.

'Where have you been? I was worried about you.' I picked him up and had a proper look at him. He seemed contented enough. I treated him with soap and water and Tineafax ointment, a cream I used for skin infections and ringworm. He protested at first, but not too wildly, then went straight outside and rolled over on the dusty ground. The next time I kept him inside for a while to give the cream a chance to work.

Jeremy joined us at Evensong one night, lying down beside Joan and me as we were kneeling. He was very good until the Psalms, when he leapt on to each of our laps in turn and set us off laughing so that in the end we reached that helpless state where we couldn't stop. One of us would say half a verse and then break down, and the other would finish it and break down themselves. It was agony until the Psalms were over.

It was the Chinese Moon festival, and Siew Mann made some special cakes – dough with a savoury inside – which she steamed. As we ate, she told us about her life before she came to Sandakan. She had grown up in Jesselton, living with an older sister who had four children. Her day would begin at 5.30 a.m., when she did the family's washing. At 7 o'clock she would leave to walk a mile for the bus, sometimes having to forgo breakfast if her duties had taken too long. School hours were from 8 a.m. to 1 p.m. and 2 to 4 p.m. She got home at 6 p.m., had a bath and a meal, then did the washing up. After that there was homework to do for four hours, and if she had exams, she would get up at 3 a.m. to revise for them.

Her father had come to Borneo from China as a young man, something that would have been impossible now as only the elderly, who were of no further use to the community, were permitted to leave.

'I have a cousin who was so desperate to leave China, he escaped fifteen months ago by swimming to Hong Kong,' she said.

'That sounds dangerous!'

'Very dangerous. He was almost there when he was picked up by a boat. The authorities contacted my father and they've allowed him to work at the Jesselton Hotel. So he is fortunate. If he is a good citizen they will let him stay and work where he likes after two years.'

'And what was he doing in China?' asked Joan.

'The same as everyone else. Most people work on communal farms, or the ones who live in towns do building work. Everyone is a labourer. All except the old and disabled work hard, from dawn till it's dark, every day.'

We asked her about religious life.

'There is little time for the church. People probably do meet secretly but they have to be careful.' She sighed. 'We all hope this regime will end soon and that people will be able to live freely.'

It was the end of September and I was starting to think about Christmas. As my posting was for three years – unless I chose to renew it – it would probably be my last Christmas in Borneo, though my first in Tongud. As I sat in the dispensary one afternoon, I began to write a list of people I needed to send a card to back home. I was stranded there with my last two patients as a violent thunderstorm had started to shake the world outside. I could feel the ground tremble with every thunderclap, and was thankful that the boys had recently repaired the dispensary roof.

I gave the men a jigsaw puzzle to pass the time. It was a novelty to them, and once they had realized what the purpose of it was, their concentration was a pleasure to witness. I kept stopping what I was doing to look across at them. Sometimes they groaned when a piece didn't fit, and we would catch each other's eye and laugh. It was one of those rare, perfect moments and I would have happily sat like that for the rest of the day.

A plague of mosquitoes bit me relentlessly as I began writing the cards that evening. They were everywhere. Cases of malaria had continued to rise in the past few weeks. The government was sending malaria spray teams to the kampongs and I hoped they would reach us soon.

It began to rain again and I moved a bucket to catch the drips. Some of our mission buildings were badly in need of repair. Roofs were usually the first to go as leaves could only withstand the weather and attack from animals and insects for a certain amount of time. At times like this we missed Andrew more than ever. But other things were being neglected, too: work had ground to a halt on the building of the new chapel. Arnold was unhappy, as the people in the kampongs had agreed to carry out this work. It was part of the deal for providing them with free healthcare and education for their children.

When we spoke to Frank, he suggested writing to the ADO and asking him to call a meeting of all the OTs when he came in November.

He also asked if I would write an article for a parish newsletter in Taunton to explain why we needed the new tele-radio they had promised to pay for.

'If you tell them something about the sort of work you do, Wendy, let them see how important it is.'

'Yes, I can do that. About 300 words?'

'Sounds perfect. And, um, if Arnold could bring it with him.'

'Frank, Arnold is leaving in an hour's time!'

'I'm sorry it's rather last minute, Wendy, but I know you're good at that sort of thing.'

Frank could charm the snakes out of the walls of our house, I mused, as I dashed back to my desk. But no one was more passionate or hard-working than he was, and I knew he would do anything for us, so it was hard to refuse him. Sometimes I wondered how Frank coped as he did, running his parish with no assistance as well as supervising the Interior Mission, which now included two other schools plus the new mission in Telupid.

Lawrence was being confirmed in Jesselton. The day before the confirmation, I asked Frank to send a telegram care of

Bishop Wong to let Lawrence know I was thinking of him. But what to say? Should I send love? Prayers? I decided on, 'Blessings & thoughts for confirmation.' I thought of him on the day by playing Swan Lake and a piano concerto he had given me. We certainly shared many interests, I thought, music being one of them. But I knew that wasn't enough. I didn't love him.

I shivered. The temperature had dropped to an unusually low 74 degrees (23 degrees Celsius), just as I was suffering from a cough and cold. I pulled on a pair of brown slacks I had never worn, an Aertex blouse with long sleeves (which I'd worn once before) and my blue cardigan and brown socks (worn occasionally).

I was only just dressed when I was interrupted by some of the boys trooping up to the house.

'Sister! Sister! We are ready!' they shouted.

Joan, who was always thinking of ways to improve the lives of her pupils, had recently bought them all plimsolls, as they otherwise went barefoot and were prone to ringworm. I had used my latest donations from supporters to buy mosquito nets for the boarding house. I had told the boys that as soon as they had prepared their beds for the nets, they could come to collect them from the dispensary. A dozen boys appeared soon after, and when I went to check I was impressed by the rotan and bamboo frames they had constructed. They squealed with joy and danced when I handed over the nets, and after giving them a talk about their importance in the fight against malaria, I hastened to repair my own.

Those who had not been ready had been told they would have to wait until Monday for theirs but, seeing them standing there, unable to keep still through excitement, I relented and went to open the dispensary to find and distribute them.

I went to the boarding house later to check that they had been put up properly and found all of the boys happily in

Newly shod: schoolboys are helped with their first shoes

bed, reading schoolbooks under their nets, though it was only 7 p.m.!

Back home, snuggled in my cardigan, I listened to Anthony preaching on Radio Sarawak – he always gave a good sermon – and thought about our stay with him, before picking up August's *She* magazine.

I had met Father Val Ticobay, a Filipino priest, and his wife, Angelita, a nurse, a few times in Sandakan before they had left to run the new mission in Telupid. We decided that it would be a good idea for Angelita to observe my work in the dispensary, and agreed that the couple would stay a few days with us. They arrived after spending several days trekking through the jungle. Father Ticobay was in a state of collapse, with a high fever, and I put him straight to bed. I suspected he might have malaria. He was perspiring heavily and vomiting all but water. I took blood slides and thought I saw the parasite, but I couldn't be totally sure.

Later, as we ate our meal, Angelita confided that she was three or four months' pregnant. Remembering my own journey to and from Telupid, on foot and by boat, I was annoyed that no one had warned them about the difficulties of the route.

Speaking to Frank over the radio I told him that when the Ticobays returned they should not attempt to walk back but should go all the way by boat via Sandakan.

'Father Ticobay is very ill, and I don't want Angelita sleeping in the open and doing dangerous walks. You know she's pregnant, don't you? And I'd like her to see Dr Willis before she returns to Telupid.'

Frank said he understood.

I wonder, I thought!

The job of the malaria spray team was to spray the walls and other indoor surfaces of houses with a pesticide called DDT, which would kill insects that came into contact with them. Joan and I got up even earlier than usual on the day our house was to be sprayed, moved everything away from the walls to the middle of the room, and covered the furniture with dust sheets. Lily and two of the girls came to help and brushed all the walls with brooms. The room was soon swirling with clouds of dust.

In the dispensary I took down the curtains and moved the chairs, tables and mats outside. When the spraying was complete, the girls helped me to wash the mats and scrub the floors with soapy water. Siew Mann rearranged the furniture

Tongud schoolgirls: Kamsiah, Helena, Fatimah and Lily

and rehung the curtains, while I washed down all the shelves. Back in the house, the girls dusted our books and replaced them on the shelf.

I noticed how the sleeves of my records were growing patches of mould. Everything was decaying and rotting. Everything was consumed, eventually, by the damp heat. I wondered how quickly a place like Tongud would be taken over by the vegetation if it were ever abandoned. Would any legacy of ours remain a hundred years from now?

Angelita was nursing her husband, and when she had time she was helping me and observing in the dispensary. One day a group of Dusuns arrived from a distant kampong and every one of them had yaws, including a mother and her one-year-old child, who both had huge lesions on their faces and bodies. Angelita had never seen the disease before, so it was fortunate she had the opportunity. I explained how, though the doctors in Sandakan had initially been resistant to my idea of treating all known contacts of yaws cases, through my persistence I was now allowed to give penicillin to them, though of course this was only possible when I was in the kampongs and had all the people together. But at least I felt I was making some headway in battling the disease.

After Evensong we went through all the drugs – their uses and doses – until 6.30 p.m. when I broke off as it was my turn to cook. Nasi goreng (an Indonesian rice dish), with jelly fluff for pudding – now there was a combination!

Samuel and I went to visit the Panglima, who was very ill with malaria and pneumonia. Dalila and another woman were sitting wailing at the entrance to his house. Dalila was rattling pieces of copper, and a basket with a piece of pig's hair in it sat beside her.

She stopped wailing when she saw me, smiled and told us to go up. She was relieved I was visiting as she knew I didn't approve of mameows. But I had heard the Panglima's congested lungs, and knew that a mameow was not going to be enough to see him through.

Inside I asked the Panglima's wife what the women outside were doing. She looked uncomfortable and said the mameow was for someone else.

We prayed for him and our other sick at Mass on Sunday morning, a service that was usually well attended by the pupils and the villagers. Today Arnold preached in Mankaak, another of the local languages. I sometimes feared that my own attempts to converse might have become an odd amalgam of

Malay and various Dusun tongues as I had picked up a lot of local words from my Tongud friends. However, I usually managed to make myself understood. We sang 'All things bright and beautiful' for the first time, which made me smile. Yet as I listened to the words, I thought how, really, they were most inappropriate for Borneo: 'The cold wind in the winter, the pleasant summer sun.'

These were sentiments that belonged to the British people and our temperate climate!

Ah well, the children were enjoying it. Their smiles were infectious and I sang with even more enthusiasm.

13

A view of the hills

October to December 1961

OT Harun came to ask me to visit a woman who he said was mad. After first checking on the Panglima, Samuel and I joined the headman in a perhau. Two boys paddled us up the Kinabatangan for about 20 minutes to a spot where most of the community were living while they brought in the harvest. As we sailed, he told me her story. Latifah's husband had left her a few weeks earlier and now she sat smoking all day, staring into space and doing no work. She rarely slept. At other times she became violent and people were afraid of her.

Latifah was very subdued in my presence. She answered my questions at first, then clammed up and refused to say more. I gave her an injection of Largactil, an anti-psychotic drug, and left some tablets and instructions for taking them with the OT, telling him that if she hadn't shown some improvement in a few days to let me know and I would take her to Sandakan.

I sat in the front of the perhau and paddled back in the blazing sun, one of the boys paddling behind me. I felt sure there was something that the OT wasn't telling me. Whenever I asked him another question he merely repeated his description of her behaviour.

I said goodbye to the Ticobays, who were leaving on *Malaikat Raphael*. Father Ticobay was still weak, but well enough to travel. I was so thankful that we had this quicker method of transport and that they would be in Sandakan in two days, even if it wasn't the most comfortable journey. I hoped they would be happy in Telupid. We had recently learnt of an officer who had been training there and had found it too lonely and asked to be relocated. Remembering Andrew, I knew that these remote locations did not suit everyone. And yet, now that I knew them so much better, I felt confident that the Ticobays would cope.

After Evensong, Arnold, Joan and I went for a walk to the top of the hill. It was a short but very steep climb and we were gasping when we reached the top. Captain Mills and his men had cleared some trees in preparation for their surveying work and, thanks to this, using my new binoculars I had the joy of seeing Mount Kinabalu from Tongud for the first time. There were other mountains in the distance, but Mount Kinabalu soared above them all. As we stood there watching, it became lost in the cloud.

I don't do this often enough, I thought. I don't take time to walk around my own surroundings. But it was easier said than done when the days went by so quickly, governed by a routine that had to be adhered to in order to make the most of the hours of daylight – six in the morning to six in the evening, all year round – and the slightly cooler hours of the early morning. Often it would be dark before I had a spare minute to myself.

I went to see Latifah again. She seemed more relaxed and said she was starting to sleep better, but she still didn't feel able to work. In the absence of the OT, she talked more freely while her two small children sat and played beside us. She told Samuel and me that her husband, Abdullah, had left her and her four children three months earlier because his second wife disliked her. He went to work on a timber camp, and when he returned he spent a night with her, and his second wife slept in the OT's house. The next day he arranged for Latifah's belongings to be put in the perhau ready to return with them all to the timber camp, but when the other wife saw what he had done she exploded, and threatened to injure her. In the end they had left her behind and, without telling her, had taken two of her children. Since then she had been experiencing deep depression and anxiety.

I advised her to attempt a little work and to try not to worry too much. I said if she could come to the dispensary every day for an injection of Cytamen, the routine might help a little. She agreed to do this, and when I left I felt more positive about the outcome.

The next day Latifah paddled to the dispensary herself. She appeared and sounded much better and was taking an interest in things. She looked round the dispensary and asked questions about some of the posters I had put up. Then she grew tearful, and said she kept dreaming about her husband, and that during the day she imagined she could see him.

'That's normal,' I said, squeezing her hand. 'It's good that you're sleeping. When you sleep your mind is dealing with some of the problems from your waking hours. And as for seeing things, well, we all imagine things sometimes.'

'That is right,' agreed Samuel. 'Sometimes when I am not with them I see Larnia and Philip before my eyes. Of course, at other times I am happy that I am not with them.'

Even Latifah managed a smile over this. She said that OT Harun sometimes gave her food, otherwise she would go out and find tapioca for herself and her children. I gave her soap, milk and salt, Farex for the little ones and, as she had been showing such interest in them, a few Christmas cards.

We were expecting a new visitor. Joan's brother, John, who was on his way home to Tasmania after working in Britain, was coming to stay with us. Joan paddled down with some of the boys to meet him, and they arrived just after Evensong.

John Goodricke was dark and bearded, and had a confident, easy manner. I gave him and Joan cold drinks before serving up fried sausages, eggs, tomatoes and tapioca chips. John said he certainly hadn't expected a fry-up! He kept us amused with tales of his exploits as a steeplejack, then Joan asked if I would play him some of my records. By the time we had listened to Beethoven's First, Eighth and Ninth symphonies, it was after midnight. John said his first night in Tongud had confounded all his expectations.

When he spent the next day observing in the dispensary and looking round the buildings of the mission and the kampong, it became obvious how useful he could be to us. He and Arnold disappeared for a couple of hours, and when they came back Arnold had a big smile on his face. Arnold had been hoping to pump water from the river up to the mission, but it was beyond any of our capabilities. It turned out that John had experience with hydram pumps, and he had offered to stay in order to install one for us. Andrew was still sorely missed, so we considered ourselves very fortunate to have found a replacement for him. John moved into the spare room in Arnold's house.

It wasn't long before, whenever a visitor asked when he had to go back to Tasmania, John was replying, 'When they don't need me here any more.'

The next morning John, Joan, Arnold and Siew Mann set off in *Malaikat Raphael* to the wedding of one of the schoolboys.

A school holiday had been declared. I closed the dispensary at lunchtime, and for the rest of that day peace reigned in Tongud. I played part of the *Messiah* and attempted to sing. There was no one to hear me, and I really put my heart into it.

I went for a walk, but that was less fun on my own, and I knew it wasn't sensible to wander too far alone.

As the hours of darkness grew nearer I began to look out for the others. I boiled two kettles of water for them to wash when they got back, and started preparing supper. When they arrived they brought back half a pot of cooked rice so I made nasi goreng for us all.

Joan nudged me as we gave John his first taste of the durian fruit.

He pulled a face. 'You eat this?'

Joan and I laughed.

'We all think it's revolting,' she said, 'but everyone has to try it.'

'Gwynnedd, who I stayed with when I first came to Borneo, is the only Westerner I know who likes it. We're still waiting to find another.'

Arnold was planning another trip. We would be away for more than a week and I was already getting anxious about it. I wasn't sure if I was physically or mentally up to it. To make matters worse, my period was due to start on the day we set off – something I wasn't sure I could bring up with Arnold.

The day before we left, Dalila came round with some maize to sell. Through Samuel I asked her what had been going on the previous night when we had heard noises and shouting and seen several figures dancing around the Panglima's house and garden, two of them holding fire torches on the end of long poles. It had looked and sounded quite spooky in the darkness, and I guessed they were frightening away evil spirits.

Dalila said it was a mameow for the Panglima, but when I went to see him later he said he hadn't seen or heard anything. Perhaps I should have learnt by now that it was best not to ask!

Just before we left, Muhammad brought his second wife to the clinic. I was horrified to see that her tonsils were so grossly enlarged that her throat and uvula were invisible.

'You should have brought her sooner,' I chided him. 'The poor thing!'

I was upset that because I was going away I wouldn't be able to administer the daily penicillin she needed. I gave her an injection of procaine penicillin and started her on Tetracycline capsules, which I hoped would be enough.

It was beautiful when Arnold, Samuel and I set off upriver in a small borrowed gobang, with two boys at the helm. It wasn't long before we had to get out and walk through the rapids; indeed, we probably spent more time on foot than we did in the canoe those first two days. Walking on the stones and boulders became quite painful after a while.

Arnold shot an owl that swooped across our path and landed on a tree nearby. It was a skinny thing and I couldn't help thinking as he plucked it that it would have been better to have left it.

He asked me to teach him the words of the Christmas carol 'I saw three ships'.

'Why that one?'

'I like it! And we are always on boats!'

We sang it several times, until Arnold was singing it back to me. He said that when he tried to translate English carols into Dusun he had trouble with the word 'Nowell' and also 'snow'. When I tried, I realized how difficult it was to describe snow to someone who had never seen it, how it felt and what it was like to walk in.

'Maybe one day, Arnold, you will visit me and see snow in England!'

He said he would like that very much.

We left the gobang and travelled on foot, passing through several kampongs – some containing just a house or two – and left messages at each to announce clinics on our return. Samuel threw me papayas from the trees so that they split open and covered me in pieces of fruit and sticky juice.

The Menokoks build their houses on the tops of hills, and one day we arrived at one in a beautiful location, with views of the mountains all around. There were four families living in the building, which was old and falling to pieces and had huge gaps in the floor. I was given a small section to myself. It had a very low roof and was screened off from the rest of house. At about seven by three feet it was just big enough to sleep in, and when I lay down I had a perfect view of a distant hill. Arnold and I had to walk some distance to have a bath, and eventually found a tiny stream with a few inches of muddy water. We managed to wash, and with some difficulty I even washed my clothes, hanging them to dry over some tapioca bushes. I went into my little hideout and wrote up my diary in peace while Arnold talked with the OT and the men. When I emerged I tried to engage the women in conversation, and admired the beadwork around their necks, in their ears and in their hair.

Samuel had been translating for Arnold, and then did the same for me in my clinic. Many of the people had goitres, and I gave them blocks of salt to add to their diet. I also treated eight people for yaws. The place swarmed with dogs, who made a deafening noise when they all began howling. No one apart from me seemed to be bothered by them.

Then we asked questions for the maternal and kampong surveys we were carrying out. I learned that the OT and his wife had three children living and that 15 had died, most of them when they were less than a year old.

I wanted to take a blowpipe back to England, and after much deliberation the people agreed to sell me an old one, as well as some poisoned darts and a bamboo holder, all for $10. They also let me have a *bongan* for $10. This bag, worn like a knapsack and conical in shape, was beautifully worked all over with plaited rotan. I put it on my back, waved to everyone and pretended I was leaving. They all laughed a lot. Then I came back, picked up the dart-holder and the blowpipe and told them I was going hunting. They roared with laughter at this. Keeping up the pretence, I walked out along a tree trunk for about 50 yards until I heard a man cough nearby, so I hastily retreated. They laughed even more when I told them why I'd come back, especially when the bemused-looking fellow returned on my heels.

I retreated to my hideout, which I now shared with a hen. The smell of dogs, hens and pigs and their excreta under the house was nauseating; indeed, the whole place was filthy. The hen gave me a curious look before flapping her wings and flying off. The sky was cloudy, and if it rained I was going to get soaked, as would everyone else in this crumbling longhouse. And yet it was a magical spot. It was so rare for me to have privacy like this when we were on our expeditions.

We arrived at our next location to find the people drunk. They had finished weeding their OT's padi, for which he gave them food and lodging, and they were now celebrating, passing round the tapai jar. Arnold felt it was too rowdy for him to attempt to speak.

'When they are worshipping the jar, nothing will stop them,' he said unhappily.

I suggested we ask the OT to order a stop to the gongs, drinking and noise so that I could hold the clinic, and by the time I had finished they might have sobered up. It seemed to work, and I marvelled at the way Arnold's talk and teaching seemed to transform the people he spoke to. They all sat and listened most reverently.

Eight of us slept on a small area of floor, like sardines, while the partying resumed. I woke at midnight. Gongs were playing; men and women were wailing and drinking heavily. After listening to this for an hour I felt desperate. It didn't help that I had a stabbing pain in my abdomen. Samuel was sitting close to where I lay, talking to one of our carriers, the latter very drunk. I asked him if he could speak to them about the noise. For about half an hour, all was silent, but I was too tense to get back to sleep. Then it all started again.

By now I was so mad I sat up and shouted, 'Shut up! Please shut up!'

This had no effect, other than a very brief, startled silence. Feeling rather foolish, I tried again using some Malay, explaining that, if I was going to run a clinic the next day and supply them with medicine, I needed to rest. The gongs stopped, and it was mainly quiet, except for a small group of people who carried on talking and singing.

I could feel the beginning of dysentery, and had never felt so relieved to be returning to Tongud. I lay back in the boat and tried to sleep, but it was no good as I had to concentrate on keeping my balance through the numerous rapids. On the way back we stopped to see the wife of Muhammad whom I had treated for the throat infection before leaving. Only his first wife was at home and she told me that my patient was well and that she was out among the padi, scaring away the birds and monkeys. She gave me four little eggs as I left.

Back in our house, aching all over, I had tea, boiled water for a hot bath and got ready for bed. I was asleep at 6 p.m.

Siew Mann brought me breakfast in bed. I thanked her, but I knew that I should only consume fluids until the dysentery had stopped. Joan popped her head round the door to say hello and ask me how I was. Later, barely able to move, I heard her preparing lunch for herself and John. I thought she might come and ask me if I needed anything, and when she didn't I dragged myself to the kitchen to fetch a drink. That evening she made Horlicks for herself and her brother, and left me to make my own.

I listened to them talking. John was outlining some of his plans for the pump, though they sounded rather technical to my ears.

I spent most of the next day in bed too, only getting up when I had to. I felt utterly miserable. When I saw Joan that evening, before I could stop myself, I exploded, telling her she was thoughtless and insensitive. She looked surprised and asked what she had done, but I had no energy for a proper conversation and staggered back to my room.

'I'm sorry,' I said when I saw her over breakfast the next day. I was feeling much better. 'The tablets I was taking make me feel depressed. I felt sorry for myself and I shouldn't have taken it out on you.'

'It's all right,' said Joan. 'I didn't think you wanted anything to eat or drink, but I should have asked anyway. I'm sorry for not looking after you better.'

'Joan, you will tell me, won't you, if I do something that annoys you? There's no point in us living so close to each other and seething over things the other one does. I'm more than happy to change my ways.'

Joan nodded. 'OK.'

'So tell me, there must be something.'

Joan thought for a moment. 'Actually, I can't think of anything.'

We both laughed. We had made up.

My patient one morning was a Muslim imam. He was a bright, curious fellow and he had been looking with interest at our pictures of Christ on the cross and asking Samuel questions. I extracted his badly decayed and broken molar. He mentioned my patient, Latifah, the woman suffering from depression, and shaking his head, said her husband was no good. I didn't think it a good idea to criticize someone I had never met, so instead said I thought it wasn't good to have more than one wife.

To my surprise he nodded resignedly. 'Lots of wives, lots of problems,' he agreed.

I had just had a bath one evening in early December when John turned up, looking tired, dirty and distressed. He had been returning in *Malaikat Raphael* with medical supplies, tools for the hydram and a large batch of post. Within five hours of Tongud the engine had stopped and the jungkung had been swept into trees and capsized. Nearly all the barang had been lost, with the exception of some furniture for the dispensary and a batch of dried milk. He and the crew had stood on branches until locals came in perhaus to rescue them. I was relieved that they were safe, and that the boat itself – though in need of repair – had been salvaged, but sad about the missing cargo, which John said had included several letters for me, and cards and presents for us all from Sister Christina. I felt the loss of the post – my much-needed contact with the rest of the world – particularly keenly.

Arnold was away for most of December for the diocesan conference. He had recently learnt that the parents of Rosemary Lim, a young woman he had told us about – though not as much as Joan and I would have liked! – had agreed to his marriage proposal to their daughter. Arnold had met Rosemary when he was a priest at St Peter's School in Saratok, and she was a teacher there. They would marry in Kuching while he was away. As soon as we heard the news, Joan fished out her record, 'Rose Marie', with its lyrics, 'Oh Rose Marie, I love you', which we both sang along to, pressing our hands to our hearts. Arnold hadn't heard the song before and found it very amusing.

In Arnold's absence, Samuel and I were holding clinics up and down the river and sharing the Christmas story in the kampongs we visited. Samuel took his radio with him, which often provided a useful distraction for our patients, though as he tended to switch it on as soon as he woke up, I had to tell him that six in the morning was really the earliest I wanted to hear it!

On one of these trips we were asked to visit a house where a wedding had just taken place, and found two men with extensive scalds. One of them, Juga, could not move. Large

Wendy and Samuel (with hat) are taken to visit the sick by schoolboy boatmen (below) and (right) share the story of the Nativity

areas of raw flesh covered most of his legs and buttocks; other parts of his legs and back were charred black and had huge blisters. A second man, though less seriously hurt, had large raw areas on his back. It had happened the previous evening when a vat of boiling water had fallen on them. Some people said the men had been fighting; others that they had been trying to stop a dog fight. I gave them drugs and dressed their wounds, then sent some men to find poles to improvise a stretcher, using two sarongs. They carried Juga to the canoe, accompanied by his wife and two small children. The other man was able to walk unaided. Juga was in agony. I did my best to make him comfortable, raising his legs and

Juga is carried along the path from the river to the dispensary

supporting them with wide bandages strung across the backs
of two of the salvaged chairs we were bringing back.

I was looking forward to Christmas, but it was going to be
a busier time than I had anticipated. We had special visitors
coming to join us: Flo and Peggy from Jesselton were making
their first trip to the interior, and many local Christians in
the area were congregating in Tongud.

On Christmas Eve people were arriving all day from their
kampongs. Samuel and I were worked off our feet as many
of them wanted to visit the dispensary, and my inpatients
needed a lot of care. But there was a delightful sense of
anticipation in the air. I prepared our temporary chapel in
the school with white curtains and vestments and arranged
for the boys to take the evening service. When I heard the
engine at around 5 p.m. I dashed down to the river to meet

the arrivals. Flo and Peggy were relieved to be on dry land, but happy and excited.

Arnold beamed as he introduced me to a small, smiling, bubbly woman: Rosemary, his new wife. I knew that she and I were going to get along.

The chapel looked beautiful on Christmas morning. The boys had decorated it with leaves, shrubs and flowers, and Siew Mann had made bamboo candlesticks for the altar as well as for our dining table. We sang carols in Dusun. The room was packed. I sat beside Juga, who had been carried in on a stretcher. Larnia, with Philip on her lap, sat on my other side. It was noisy with chatter, babies crying, and the occasional sound of spitting, but still a lovely service.

Just before 9 a.m. we tuned in to Telupid to exchange Christmas greetings with the Ticobays.

'Please come for lunch!' said Angelita, so we said we'd get into our private plane and be there in a jiffy, and asked them to drop in for tea!

We had breakfast of grapefruit, eggs and fresh bread. Then we opened our presents – there were gifts from my parents, Joe and Rhoda, and others from the mission staff.

I went to see my patients then tuned in to Sandakan to speak to Frank, Sister Christina and Jean. Meanwhile, the two skinny chickens I had bought from the kedai – I had given a third to Samuel – were in the oven, and dinner preparations had begun. Joan and Siew Mann prepared the potatoes, carrots and long beans, Peggy iced the cake and Flo helped with everything else. Joan and I had already made a start on bread sauce, apple sauce, gravy, and sage and onion stuffing.

The table in our little house had never looked more festive, with one of my pink sheets masquerading as a tablecloth, red flowers from my garden, candles, and the crackers I had been sent from home at every place setting. Closing my eyes and smelling the roast dinner, I might have been back in Northumberland if it wasn't for the heat.

'We don't do so badly here, do we?' I said, when we were finally all sitting down.

'I certainly wasn't expecting to hear anyone say, "Pass the stuffing, please,"' added John.

The chicken dinner was followed by plum pudding and brandy sauce, and when everyone said they had eaten far too much, I realized it really was just like Christmas at home.

In the afternoon we went back to the chapel to watch the Nativity play, followed by the admission of about 50 catechumens. Supper was soup made from the chicken pickings, fruit salad and tinned cream, and later there was Christmas cake. After attending to my patients, Joan and I went to the boarding house and found it bursting with people. Three boys helped us to carry down the boxes full of presents, and we gave them out to those who were there. Each boy received a sarong, a towel, a toothbrush, soap and two handkerchiefs. They were practical gifts, but as most of them had never received a Christmas present before, their gratitude was a pleasure to behold.

It had been a special day, but we had an important journey to prepare for. Juga needed hospital treatment, and we would deliver Siew Mann, Flo and Peggy back to town at the same time. After that I would be travelling to stay with Miss Waites in Jesselton.

We set off the next morning in a borrowed gobang. It was a tight fit with us four women, Juga on his stretcher, Samuel to assist me, and two boys manning the boat. At the last minute Larnia decided that she and Philip would come as well. This wasn't going to be the most comfortable journey, I thought. I only hoped it would be a swift one.

14

A maze of rivers

December 1961 to February 1962

It began to rain and continued all day. Those in the front of the boat – especially poor Peggy – got soaked. The boat was leaking, too, so I spent a good deal of time baling water out of the back. I kept Juga as dry as I could by covering him with a sheet of plastic.

We stayed that night in a Chinese store in Pintasan where we were given a room at the back containing two wooden benches. Flo and Peggy slept on one bench, Siew Mann on a camp bed, and Juga and I shared the other bench, under my mosquito net.

About an hour after setting off the next morning we hit a huge log that was submerged in the river. It knocked the transom and engine almost right off the boat. Fortunately a launch was close by and its crew lent us a hammer and nails so that we could reattach the transom and continue to Lamag, where *Malaikat* was waiting for us with her brand new 30 hp engine.

Malaikat was going well; it felt quick after the less-powerful engine of the gobang. We had planned to spend the night at the OT's house in Abai. Flo and I were sitting talking when I thought I recognized Abai, and expected Simon to stop. When he carried on I thought nothing of it, assuming I had been mistaken. A little later I asked him if he knew where we were but got no answer. It was dark now and heavy rain was falling through a thin mist. We kept entering narrow channels and having to reverse out of them.

With a sinking feeling, I realized that we were lost. At 12.30 a.m. Simon stopped the engine and tied the boat to a nipa palm tree. The animal noises we heard sounded very close, and more eerie in the mist, though the only creatures that bothered us were mosquitoes, which attacked constantly. In the cabin, where I slept with Juga, rain splashed through the gaps in the windows.

We set off at 6.30 a.m. I could see Simon was worried, but he wasn't saying much. The rest of the party had slept on deck and were soaked. I made tea for us all and it tasted distinctly salty, so I guessed we were somewhere near the Trusan. As we were drinking it there was a sudden bang and a flash of flame leapt from the engine. The cabin filled with smoke and oily fumes. I dashed inside, opened the windows and fanned the smoke while reassuring poor Juga, who lay in the midst of this, unable to move, and no doubt wondering if he was going to survive this journey.

Simon informed me that a vital part of the engine had broken and there was nothing he could do about it. We were in serious trouble – lost in a narrow river where, for all we knew, other boats might never pass. Everyone knew that this part of the coast was like a maze.

We had two main options. If we tied up at the side and waited to be found we might keep ourselves from danger, but we could be there for days; in fact, we might never be found at all. What's more, we would soon run out of food, and even sooner run out of drinking water. The second option was to drift and hope to be discovered by a passing launch – but we might land on a sandbank or be carried out to sea, which was too rough for a little launch like *Malaikat*, with or without an engine.

Although it was far from satisfactory, we decided to drift, and to hope and pray that we might come across another boat before reaching the sea.

We drifted slowly, painfully slowly. The rain – which had carried on all night – stopped for a while and we put the wet clothes and bedding on the roof to dry. When it began to rain again we collected it from the canvas roofing in plastic bags and managed to partially fill the water carrier and bottles.

'Why is the water blue?' asked Samuel, and we discovered that it was because of Peggy's wet cardigan which was lying on the roof.

Peggy and I tried standing on the roof with a sheet, which we hoped would act as a sail and get us moving more quickly, but there was no breeze.

After we had been drifting for two hours the river opened out, like an estuary, and we caught sight of a small boat a long way off. We all waved and shouted but it didn't see us and eventually disappeared.

I could see the fear and disappointment on the faces of the others, and I felt pretty despondent myself.

'We've seen one, so there are sure to be more boats,' I said as cheerfully as I could, wondering if I really believed what I was saying.

By now we were singing 'It's a long way to Tipperary' and 'Land of hope and glory' to try to stay positive. Peggy made a flag to wave using a piece of stick and a scarf, but there was no one to see it.

It was mid morning when someone glimpsed a launch in the distance. Flo and I got on to the roof and, thinking back to my days as a Girl Guide – how useful they had proved to be so far! – I made the SOS Morse code signal with my torch over and over again.

I was hungry – we were afraid to eat too much of our food – and even more thirsty. I was anxious for baby Philip, though for now he seemed oblivious to our woes and was sleeping on Larnia's lap. It felt like a matter of life and death that we attract this boat's attention.

'It's coming nearer!' cried Flo.

I wasn't sure.

'It's taking its time if it is,' said Peggy.

The boat did seem a little closer, yet it wasn't moving in our direction. It can't have seen us, I thought. A missed opportunity. I felt sick with despair. How long would we have to wait for another?

Peggy was waving her flag madly and shouting at the top of her voice.

After what seemed like ages, the boat began to head towards us. The relief was terrific. As it got closer we saw that it was a launch belonging to Tann's timber camp. I don't think I'd ever been so happy to see a stranger than I was to see Mr Albert Tann. He told us that we were five hours south of the Kinabatangan. We had drifted a long way off course. He offered to take me to their camp, which was about three hours' away, and from there we could travel to another camp and contact our friends in Sandakan by radio. The next day we would return for the other passengers and they would take us to our destination.

Flo offered to come with me and, after giving Peggy instructions about Juga's drugs and asking Samuel to take care of him, we rather reluctantly left our party. Before we did, the launch towed *Malaikat* to a safe part of the river and tied her to a tree.

Mr Tann told Flo and me that his crew had been afraid to come near us as they feared we might be pirates. When they had used binoculars and seen women on board, they thought it might be an elaborate trick and were still reluctant, but Mr Tann had insisted they go closer. As they did, one of the men recognized *Malaikat* as being a Kinabatangan mission launch.

We realized we had been very lucky. Mr Tann showed us a recent newspaper report about a launch carrying a tractor that had disappeared, never to be seen again. In a recent raid on their own camp, 25 pirates had announced their arrival by firing two shots in the air, whereupon most of the workers had fled. The manager had been held up at gunpoint and forced to hand over the safe, after which, knowing that it contained only $80, he had fled, fearing for his safety. After looting the camp the pirates travelled to another, where they made off with $20,000 before escaping in their powerful longboat. There was little the victims could do as neither company was due to radio its office in Sandakan on that day.

He also told us how dangerous it was that we had no anchor, and how we might have been swept out to sea.

After reaching the camp we had a two-mile walk, barefoot and in thick mud, along the timber railway to radio Frank and explain our predicament.

Back in Mr Tann's camp Flo and I had a bath in a sort of cubby hole with no door. It felt like being in The Ritz! Our host gave us a meal and insisted we take his room. It was only 9 p.m. but we were both exhausted. Flo slept on Mr Tann's bed and I used my lilo and my net which I had brought with me. I wished I hadn't bothered as they both stank of urine from the first night, when Juga's urinal had tipped over and soaked all my bedding.

Before he left us, Mr Tann removed a large dagger from underneath his pillow and offered it to Flo.

'No thank you,' she said, and he shrugged and took it with him, after shutting and barring all the windows. Pirates or no pirates, we opened one of them when he had gone, to help some of the smell from my bedding to escape.

Our abandoned passengers were very pleased to see us when the crew took us back the next morning – no one more so than Juga. The timber camp's main launch took us to Sandakan, while a smaller one towed *Malaikat.*

I left Juga in safe hands at the hospital, and arrived back at the compound just in time to see Sister Christina, who was flying home to the UK as her mother was very ill. As there had been talk of the sisters in Sandakan following her and spending a year at the mother house in Devon, I realized with sadness that it might be a long time before we would meet again.

'I could get used to this,' I thought, as I took a long soak in Miss Waites's smart bathroom in her modern Jesselton apartment. She was at work and had told me to make myself at home. On my bedside table I had a reading lamp, a radio and a pile of nursing magazines.

The next morning the *amah* (maid) brought me orange juice, followed by breakfast in bed. I discovered it was Miss Waites's birthday so went to town to buy her a gift, and that evening we had a dinner party. But I was still exhausted after my recent ordeal and was glad when she suggested I retire early.

The next day was another lazy one. Miss Waites dropped me off at the golf club, where I spent the time swimming and writing letters in the delightfully cool clubhouse. No one knew me there, and there was something liberating about having no responsibilities to anyone and being left alone.

I went to the Secretariat with Miss Waites the following day to meet Dr Clapham, Director of Medical Services, and then to the hospital for a ward round with the surgeon Dr Fozdar

Time to relax: Wendy on the beach with Sheila (left) and Flo (kneeling), and with Andrew, Joan and Arnold celebrating a birthday in Tongud

and a visit to the outpatients department. A few days later I would assist Dr Fozdar during an emergency operation on a perforated gastric ulcer. All the time I was observing closely and making notes.

A group of us went to Flo's for dinner one night. Tongud had made a big impression on her, but of course the biggest story was our journey back to Sandakan.

'We felt rather like Bobbie in *The Railway Children* when she had to wave her petticoat to get the train to stop, didn't we, Wendy?' she said cheerfully. 'It's certainly the biggest adventure I've had.'

'We wanted a different Christmas, and we got one,' added Peggy.

Father Burn said that we would be dining out on the story for years.

Miss Waites shared a small boat with Miss Brigstocke, a field officer for the Red Cross, and one day they took me sailing to a glorious island. On the way we waved to Dr and Mrs Clapham, who passed us on a smart-looking yacht. It was a dream of a location: soft white sands, clear green water, plenty of trees for shade. I had several swims before we drank our beer and ate our picnic lunch. In the afternoon we sailed to another island where I tried my hand at fishing until my hook got broken on the coral. Miss Waites had more luck and landed an eel. Miss Brigstocke's amah lit a fire and made tea and we had another swim. At 6 p.m. a storm was brewing and we left just as the sea was getting rough. We got drenched on the way back and were cold and shivering when we landed.

My ten days in Jesselton flew by and I was sorry to say goodbye to my generous hostess, who had now become a friend.

Back in Sandakan, there was shopping to do for the dispensary, and I spent several hours in Dr Willis's surgery learning about diagnoses of different diseases. I encountered Captain Mills again and he invited me to lunch. Tall and good-looking, Rob was easy to talk to and seemed genuinely interested in me – not just me the Tongud nurse, but me as a person, someone who had had a life before Borneo. I was flattered. He said that if I could wait until he returned from a trip to Singapore, he could take me back upriver on the survey boat. It was a rather loose arrangement, and I did begin to wonder if I had misunderstood it as the days went by and I heard nothing from him. But I was stranded in Sandakan anyway until *Malaikat* was fixed, so I kept busy, and waited.

When he returned two weeks later he announced he would be leaving the next morning, 2 February. It didn't take me long to pack, and I got myself and my belongings to the quayside at 9.30 a.m. There I found a small launch full to the brim with nine men and their barang and hardly a spare inch between them. My heart sank. This wasn't what I'd envisaged. Furthermore, they were only going as far as Lamag, and would be making overnight stops on the way.

As I was waiting for Rob to arrive, wondering what to do, John Goodricke arrived on *Malaikat*, saying that the engine was repaired and he would be returning to Tongud the next day. I knew it was more sensible for me to wait and travel back with him rather than to set off on a boat with strange men and very little room, so reluctantly removed my barang from Rob's boat.

Rob looked most disappointed when he turned up and I told him of my decision. He said he had been looking forward to my company. As I took a taxi back to St Monica's, I suddenly felt unhappy, and uncertain as to whether I'd done the right thing. And I was annoyed, too, that I was feeling like this. What was going on? I was returning to Tongud, as I had done dozens of times before, and hadn't expected to upset anyone – let alone myself – in the process. I felt as if I was a terrible nuisance – a woman of no fixed abode, always relying on other people. Sister Florence told me not to be so foolish when I shared these thoughts with her but, even so, I felt miserable and slept very little that night.

As expected, the novices were going to join Sister Christina in England for a year, and the next day was their last at school before their departure. Perhaps the change of plan had been for the best, I thought, for it was an occasion I wouldn't have wanted to miss. I joined them at a staff coffee party, followed by an assembly where the children presented them with dozens of bunches of flowers tied with ribbon.

The young women were so excited, so enthusiastic, so full of laughter when anyone suggested that they might not find the British climate to their liking, that I forgot my own concerns for a while.

'They say there is air-conditioning on the streets of England,' one of the party guests said, looking to me to confirm it.

I was puzzled for a few seconds. 'Oh,' I replied, cottoning on, 'I think you'll find that's just the British weather!'

On the journey back the river was fuller than I had ever seen it and the strong current hampered our progress. We sailed past flooded houses, and found ourselves level with the tops of banana trees. When we reached Lamag we realized we were sailing on to the football field. My heart gave a little leap when I saw Rob in the rest house with Mr Roberts, the ADO. We spent several hours chatting that evening, during which

I think we both felt that something was happening between us. I knew now that I had not been imagining things earlier, or reading too much into his cultured, polite manner.

I hadn't expected to find myself falling in love in Borneo. But was it a bad thing? I decided that, provided I carried on with my work to the best of my ability, it wasn't doing anyone any harm, even if it was causing my emotions to fluctuate in a way that hadn't happened for a long time! I spent most of the rest of the journey back to Tongud thinking about Rob.

Everywhere we passed we saw the effects of flooding. People had lost belongings which had been swept into the river. Simon, who had come to meet us with a gobang in Lamag, stopped to visit his sister, whose husband had been electrocuted while he had been in the water. I thought how life could be here one minute and gone the next. We owed it to ourselves to live our lives as fully as possible. It seemed suddenly very clear that I should seize this unexpected chance with both hands and not let it go.

15

Signals

February to March 1962

Arnold was worried about Rosemary. I had hardly had a chance to get my foot in the door and unpack when he came to tell me she had a pain in her chest and a headache. I found her in bed, where she complained of a tenderness in her left breast and a constant feeling of sickness. After examining her, I told her that all her symptoms pointed to pregnancy, and I could see the fear leaving her face.

'Of course! Oh, Wendy, I am so foolish! I was worried it might be something serious.'

I was more worried about another patient, the schoolboy David, whom I was very fond of. He had returned from his kampong after the Christmas vacation with a high temperature and an infected arm. His right arm was nearly three times its normal size – tense and inflamed, and with oedema of the hand. It was already getting late when I saw him in the boarding house but I felt that I couldn't leave him overnight. I admitted him to the dispensary and prepared for surgery, using a pressure lamp hung on the wall at the head of the bed for light. It was difficult getting into the vein of his left arm to give the Pentothal, but I eventually managed. I made an incision near the right elbow and pus gushed out. I made it a bit bigger and inserted a drainage tube and one nylon stitch. The Pentothal soon wore off, which wasn't pleasant for David or for us. I applied a dressing and settled him for the night. His friend

Christopher, the son of an OT from a neighbouring kampong, stayed with him.

Samuel and I were supposed to be going to Sinoa to hold
a clinic while Arnold and the boys carried on to Tangkulap
to bring back furniture for the dispensary in the shop's boat.
I knew that Rob was in Sinoa with his men, which made the
prospect doubly appealing, but when the time came I felt
unable to leave David, who still had a fever.

A few days later, after tea, I heard Arnold calling me, and
when I popped my head out the door, Rob was standing
beside him and asking if he could stay in the dispensary. It
was a lovely surprise and I felt very happy. I hadn't spoken
about him to Arnold and I wondered if he could read the
pleasure on my face.

By now David was sitting up and doing jigsaw puzzles. I
watched the way Rob and his men made a fuss of him when
they weren't busy, and how David lapped up the attention.

The next day a one-year-old child was brought in, dying of
gastroenteritis. David was well enough to be discharged, and
the infant and her parents – who also had a one-month-old
baby – moved in. I managed to stop the child's diarrhoea
and vomiting, but by evening she had collapsed and was
having difficulty breathing. Arnold baptized her. I gave her
Coramine, Ephedrine, and later chloral hydrate. Then a
dreadful night began during which – as the mother lay on the
bed, wailing intermittently – the father and I squatted on
the floor, supporting the baby to ease her breathing. At one
point a huge roundworm, six inches in length, escaped from
one nostril. Her respiratory passages seemed to be blocked

by worms and it was distressing watching, hour after hour, while she gasped for breath.

The child died at 5.30 a.m. on the morning of my birthday, and there was more wailing and weeping. After laying her out, I fetched Arnold, who spoke gently to the parents about Christian beliefs about death. It was wonderful to witness the calm and peace that descended on them. We arranged for her to have a service and be buried beside Sawal. As her body lay on the bed, a white cloth was wrapped around her head, and into a clenched fist her father put a rolled-up $1 note. Then he opened a packet of cream crackers and put one cracker into the other fist. The men made a coffin out of planks, which was carried to the chapel for a service, and then we all processed to the grave singing a Dusun hymn. The coffin was lowered down by rotan and, while Arnold led prayers, the father passed the child's belongings to a man, who laid them alongside the coffin. They consisted of a thermos flask with the top removed, a feeding bottle half full of milk, a half-used tin of condensed milk, and the wood and spring used for hanging a sarong cradle – a sort of Dusun baby bouncer. There was no weeping during the service and burial.

'It hasn't been much of a birthday for you, has it?' said Joan when I got home.

I shrugged. It was all part of a day's work, but I felt very sad. I tried to rest that afternoon but found it hard to sleep.

Arnold and Rosemary, our new teacher – a Filipino called Julius – and Rob joined us for dinner. We ate the little black hen the Panglima had given us; it was rather tough. Mum had left me a fruit cake, which Joan had iced and decorated with two flowers as a surprise.

After eating we played whist until late, sipping brandy and ginger.

Mission to serve: Joan, her brother John, Frank, Arnold, Bishop Wong, Julius and Wendy

I had said goodbye to our other guests and was seeing Rob out when he said, 'Come and look at the moon.'

I followed him away from the house. Suddenly he stopped walking and pulled me into his arms.

'I'd like to give you a special present, Wendy,' he whispered into my hair.

He kissed me.

We went to sit on a pile of logs on the floor of what was to be Arnold's new house. He talked of wanting to marry me.

'Do you think it might work, Wendy? I know we've got our differences, but I think deep down we share similar values. I'd even bet that we probably didn't have such different upbringings.'

He was a home counties public schoolboy from an illustrious family. Even the way he spoke reminded me that our lives were very different. Moreover, my Christian faith was the most important part of my life and I didn't think I could marry someone who didn't share that with me.

There was something else, too: he was planning to emigrate to New Zealand.

'They say it's a fine country, especially for Brits like us! A good place to start afresh and bring up a family. We're not so far away here so I've booked a flight to Wellington when my leave comes up in April so that I can go and see the place and make my mind up. If I do like it, and if I can find a job there, would you consider moving there with me?'

A fine rain was now falling and the mosquitoes were biting viciously, but in this unexpected romantic moment, anything seemed possible.

As I walked back to the house I felt giddy with excitement. Something was starting, and I knew that, in spite of my reservations, I didn't want it to stop. It wouldn't be easy, but people had surmounted greater obstacles to be together. There was no doubt that we were attracted to each other physically, but were we really destined to be together for the rest of our lives – to wake up together, eat together, share good times and bad times? That was something to be discovered in the weeks ahead.

Rob and I talked more about marriage and the Christian marriage service the following day. After the night before I felt rather worn out by it all. I sensed he prided himself on his unorthodox views on religion. He certainly knew his Bible, but had his own interpretation of it. Gosh, he could be annoying at times!

When he left a day later we agreed to meet whenever possible. He would be returning to Tongud to work and, as his office was in Sandakan, opportunities should be plentiful. I waved him and his party off, feeling slightly relieved that I would not have him as a distraction.

I began medical examinations on all the schoolchildren. Samuel helped by administering doses of antepar syrup. I had been able to buy this cure for worm infections with donations from home, as some of the cheaper drugs the government supplied me with were not always as successful. This was followed by the first injection of the triple antigen (for diphtheria, whooping cough and tetanus), which caused many of them to limp out of the dispensary looking very sorry for themselves.

'When I've finished the boys' medicals I'll start pulling their rotten teeth out,' I told Joan over lunch.

She put down her knife and fork. 'Thank you so much, Wendy. There am I, trying hard to get more of them to come to school, and you're doing your best to scare them off!'

'Don't worry, I'll supply false teeth,' I replied. 'Oh, can you imagine it?!' And at that thought we both got the giggles and couldn't eat again until we had composed ourselves.

On the way to visit a patient, Samuel and I watched the schoolboys catch a snake from the top of a coconut palm using a ring of fine rotan on the end of a very long pole. Lassoing it about four inches from the head, they tightened the noose and were able to pull the snake down.

'It's poisonous,' they told us, as one boy cut off its head. It was a handsome creature, about nine feet long with black and yellow markings. They were going to eat it.

Arnold teases a boy
with a lump of ice

I should have grown used to it, but it was still a shock to see these boys to whom I sometimes taught English, and whose wounds I tended – some of them as young as seven years old – behaving like hunters. These were the boys who giggled when I put on a funny voice, who threw themselves with gusto into our country-dancing sessions, and who tried – and often failed – to be brave when I had to treat them. They had little concept of the Western ideal of child-hood, though they were all playful and had a good sense of humour. I remembered their squeals and giggles when one day Arnold had teased them with the ice from my fridge.

'Fadder! Fadder! No!' they cried, some laughing so hard they couldn't move to resist it.

Two weeks later, Arnold declared Ash Wednesday a holiday and told me of his Lenten plans for his pupils. I had to intervene. He was proposing that they go without breakfast every day and abstain from meat on Wednesdays and Fridays. I reminded him firmly that these were growing children, whose diet was not particularly good to begin with. I told him that skipping breakfast was most certainly not advisable and asked him to reconsider.

When I had been in Jesselton with Miss Waites I had seen Bishop Wong and discussed the possibility of staying in Tongud for another tour. I had told him that I was undecided, and we agreed that provided cover could be found, I would go on furlough in October and let him know my decision as soon as I could. Our radio contact was unreliable these days (we were still waiting for the new radio we had been promised), and we were often unable to send out messages ourselves, though if we were lucky we could hear them.

One morning I heard Frank clearly for the first time in a while. He had a message for me from the bishop to say that an American Peace Corps nurse would be stationed in Tongud from August, so I could go on leave as planned. Part of me was relieved – I was longing for the north-east winds of Northumberland, for the company of my old friends – but I felt sad, too, to think that one day I would have to leave what I had started here.

Joan and John were setting off to buy ponies. I knew that Arnold had his doubts about this, and I did too. Why did we need ponies in Tongud? This was not their natural habitat. The local people had never seen horses before, let alone knew what to do with them. But John had his answers – three of them – and John was a practical man. First, it was a long way by river to Sandakan, and petrol was expensive. As there was talk of the track from Tongud to Telupid being cleared, we would be able to ride to Telupid and make the shorter boat journey to Sandakan from there. Second, the ponies would keep down the grass, which grew coarse and difficult to cut if not regularly maintained – a time-consuming task. Third, their manure would help to fertilize the poor soil.

I waved the party off in the rain. The Goodrickes took with them two boys from Primary Five – Jali and Stephen – who were going to act as interpreters and help to bring the ponies back. That was the last we would see of them all for several weeks.

Every day the rain was heavy. The boys had renewed the sticks that formed our chicken house, which had been leaking badly. To complete it they had needed a board across the doorway, for which I gave them a wooden box which had contained medical supplies. Now I smiled every time I saw it, as I read on the entrance, 'Tongud Dispensary'.

As I fed the chickens after breakfast one morning I fell down in the mud – my clean white dress was filthy. To add insult to injury, while I was in there I was stung on the chest by a huge insect and the area swelled up instantly. I went into the bathroom to change and wash. As I reached for the towel, a scorpion fell out of it and landed on my foot and then quickly disappeared between the slats. I screamed but there was nobody to hear me. I went under the house to find it and kill it, but it had disappeared. It was going to be one of those days.

There had been a serious outbreak of cholera in Sandakan in recent months and I heard on Radio Sabah that medical teams were coming up the Rivers Kinabatangan and Labuk to the interior with anti-cholera injections. I decided to have a campaign of my own to use my stocks of the vaccine.

With Jeremy on my lap, I wrote a letter to OT Harun in Malay, asking him to inform everyone that I would be giving anti-cholera injections on Monday and Tuesday mornings.

I was in the dispensary when I heard a powerful engine. The surveyor Peter Warner appeared, stayed for coffee, and then left just as Rob arrived. We spent much of the day together and, as Joan was away, talked long into the night.

I had hordes of patients the next morning, including 80 who turned up for their cholera vaccination. I was impatient for the session to be over so that I could see Rob again. After a short rest I went up the hill to find him, and stayed as he tried to make contact with Peter, who was on the Mankawago Hill. Surveying was so different from anything I had ever encountered; it gave me a small thrill to hear Peter speaking to us from the summit to tell us that the instruments were working well. Or perhaps whatever Rob was doing would have given me the same thrill, and I was happy just to be close to him! The men had a conversation on something that worked like a telephone, then Rob read masses of numbers off the radar-type machine.

I went back down for a bath, supper and to write my diary, then sat reading Tolstoy until midnight, hoping Rob would finish surveying and come to join me. When he didn't appear, I went back up the hill with a thermos of coffee. He wasn't there, but there were signs that he was still working so I left the flask and a note.

We had several visitors over the next few days, including David Hutchinson, an agricultural officer, and someone from the Malayan Rubber Fund Board. I showed them round the school and dispensary and took them to see the flourishing fruit and vegetable gardens and the rubber tree terraces.

One afternoon I went up the hill to act as Rob's assistant as he had had to send his Chinese assistant to Tinka Hill to see why no messages were coming from there. There was too much cloud to see the hills, so we sat and talked in the tent. Mr Hutchinson came up to relieve me so that I could feed the hens, then I packed up some food, a rug and my tape recorder and headed back.

It rained for most of the evening and night, so we couldn't do much work. I cooked a meal on the Primus for us all, and we talked and amused Rob's men – Ibans from Sarawak – with my tape recorder. They were very shy about being recorded themselves. Eventually we all stretched out to try to sleep while the men took turns to keep watch for the rain and clouds to disappear.

I awoke at 5.50 a.m. to look at the hills in their bluey splendour. The light at that time of day was almost magical. I gathered up my things and went back to the house to get breakfast ready.

Back up the hill that afternoon the clouds cleared and we saw a light flashing from Mankawago. We waited for more than an hour, and then one began to flash from Tinka. Peter's light went out for a while and there was an anxious wait for both to contact us at the same time. I helped Rob by using the telescope to observe the Morse signals sent by the others, while he used mirrors and the sun to flash messages back to them. After that he looked through the telescope and called out numbers, which I wrote down in his book. This went on for an hour in the blazing sun. Finally we sent messages to say the operation was over and the others could leave their locations and move to the next hill. We packed up and descended, too hot and tired to eat, but talked long into the night.

I wrote to tell my parents that I had met someone very special, who might be the man I would marry.

16

Perfect days

March to May 1962

Rob left and we arranged to meet in Sandakan when I would be there for Easter. When I wasn't working I was reading a lot of Tolstoy, whom Rob had recommended. Tolstoy had become a fervent believer in non-violence and, after finishing *The Kingdom of God and Peace Essays*, I realized that I, like Tolstoy, was a Christian pacifist. I wanted to recommend a book to Rob that I hoped might have a similar influence on him and wondered what he would think of Billy Graham. I had been to see the American evangelist with my parents a few years earlier on one of his first UK rallies, and he had made a big impression on me with his direct challenge to accept Jesus as one's personal saviour. Having been a High Church Anglican during the time I worshipped at Newcastle Cathedral, I was (and am today) equally happy with evangelical styles of worship.

The day before the Easter break I was in the dispensary all day and didn't stop until 6 p.m. I had almost 200 patients, most of them for the cholera vaccine, so it was a relief to board our newly repaired *Malaikat Raphael* and have no real obligations for the two days of travelling.

I received a lovely welcome in Sandakan from Sheila Merryweather, who was on her own in the boarding house. We had previously met in Jesselton and she was now teaching in St Monica's, which had a new head, as Sister Florence was now doing mission work in Sapi. Sheila took me to meet some other newcomers: Father Arthur Stally and his wife, Ann. Arthur would be Frank's replacement when Frank left Sandakan to return to ministry in the UK in October, at the same time that I was leaving.

The Ticobays were also in Sandakan for Easter. Angelita had had her baby and I was asked to be baby Cedric's god-mother at his baptism on Easter Day.

I had expected to hear from Rob. When there had been no sign of him after a few days, I went to the survey office to leave him a letter. On my way out I caught sight of him in the reading room. He told me he'd been very busy and had no car. I invited him and Peter to join Sheila and me for dinner that night. I wanted to do something special, and decided on roast beef, roast potatoes, sprouts and carrots, with jelly and fruit for dessert. The looks on the men's faces made it all worthwhile. Rob told me he would be busy for the next two days but promised to ring me as soon as he could.

When they had gone, I finally had time to read a letter from home. Mum told me how thrilled she and my father were to hear about Rob. I'd wondered what their reactions would be and, as so often happened, was surprised by them. Mum even enclosed a letter for me to give him.

Frank had been trying to contact Joan and John, who hadn't been heard of since they had set off to buy the ponies a month earlier. One morning I went to the radio and heard Joan speaking from Telupid.

'It's been such an adventure for the boys!' she exclaimed. 'They both said they were scared in the plane when we took off from Sandakan, but once we were in the air they were worried that we weren't going fast enough! When we got to Jesselton, Father Burn took them under his wing while John and I were making enquiries about the ponies – they even met the Governor at the Yacht Club. Poor Stephen, in his innocence, decided to pick up a jellyfish when he was swimming. Luckily, he wasn't stung too badly.'

But, in spite of her enthusiasm, it had been difficult and dangerous. They had faced a frightening journey by jeep to Tambunan in the dark, mud and rain. There they had bought four ponies and began the 80-mile trek to Paginatan via Ranau. The ponies had never carried a saddle before, so they bucked madly at first and the barang went flying all over the place. From Paginatan, they wanted to follow the Japanese trail to Telupid, but no one knew the way, and the risk of getting lost was too great. Instead, the Dusuns there made them two rafts out of bamboo, lashing them together with rotan, and penning the ponies in tightly so that they could not move or be thrown about. There had been rapids, big rocks and whirlpools to negotiate, and their guides had admitted to being frightened at times, having never transported animals in this way before. They still had the 40-mile trek from Telupid to Tongud ahead, along a track that wasn't properly cleared.

'Oh, Joan!' was all I could manage to say.

When Rob didn't get in touch when I expected him to, I thought he might be waiting for me to pick him up, so I hopped in the car and visited his office. He was nowhere to be seen. An Iban said he was very busy. Disappointed, I went back to the boarding house. Half an hour later, he appeared.

After a cold drink we motored to Batu Sapi, a place I had visited once with the sisters. We had to walk for about a mile along a muddy, wet path through a rubber garden to reach a patch of sand where trees provided welcome shade from the fierce sun. The tide was in so there wasn't much beach, but we had what was there all to ourselves. It felt a long way from the town. The only sound was the hum and buzz of insects. I went behind a tree to change into my bathing costume.

'Are you coming for a swim?' I asked.

Rob confessed that he hadn't brought his trunks.

When I expressed surprise, he said, 'Well, I seem to remember I was supposed to be working. You are proving to be a big distraction, Wendy. Though a delightful one!'

I ran into the beautiful water. I had never felt happier. This was the life! How long could it go on? Couldn't we stay here, like this, with everything uncomplicated, forever?

I was aware that Rob was watching me as I swam. As I walked out of the sea he took a photo of me, dripping with water.

'You are like a goddess from the deep,' he said.

Laughing, I flicked water at him, whereupon he tried to grab my leg and pull me over.

We had just finished our picnic when we heard voices. I looked up, and to my surprise saw Arthur and Ann Stally and a group of young Chinese people marching towards us.

I felt a little embarrassed, as if I had been caught in the act, though the act of what I wasn't sure. But no one in the party seemed surprised to see Rob and me.

'We followed your footsteps,' said Father Stally. 'Hope you don't mind the intrusion, but I promise we won't disturb you for long.'

We said that they were most welcome to join us.

True to their word, they left before we did, and as we walked back we saw that one of them had drawn on the sand two intertwined hearts with an arrow going through them.

The next day I was looking for Majang, our boatman, and went to ask Father Stally if he knew where he was. But before I could say anything he beamed and clasped my hand.

'Congratulations! I am so pleased to see you're a normal woman!'

'I hope you didn't think I was abnormal,' I replied, trying to make a joke of it. Father Stally looked so delighted that it was hard not to smile back.

He said he'd been sorry to think of Joan and me in the most isolated mission station, two young women 'at the right sort of age for marrying and having children'.

'You don't want to miss these opportunities, Wendy. Sometimes they only happen once.'

After I had spoken to Majang, Father Stally and I sat in a shady part of the garden, sipping lemonade.

'You're a very valuable member of the team, Wendy,' he went on, 'and I hope you don't mind my saying this when we haven't known each other long, but you're not indispensable at Tongud. None of us is indispensable. I know from Frank what wonderful work you're doing there, and believe me, no one wants to lose you, but if you leave to get married the work will carry on – thanks to what you've started.'

I felt cheered by the conversation as I went to buy some fruit and fillings for our sandwiches. Rob picked me up at 11.30 and we went for a drive, stopping by a rubber garden where we found a shady spot for a picnic. We left a couple of hours later when it began to rain.

There followed more days of picnics and beach trips, sometimes just the two of us, sometimes with our friends. One day we saw the Resident, Mr Wookey, with his wife and some friends in a new jet speedboat. I chatted to Mrs Wookey for a while, and her husband told me he would be coming to Tongud for Tamu, which was approaching once again.

I took Rob to the airport for his trip to New Zealand and gave him a letter to read on the plane, in which I set out my hopes and aspirations. As I kissed him goodbye, I was relieved to find that I felt happy and confident that – whatever happened – things would turn out for the best.

As Sheila and I were spending a lot of time together I shared my feelings for Rob with her. She seemed happy for me, though I sensed she had her reservations. One afternoon while I was writing letters she teased me by grabbing one of them and pretending to read it. I went chasing after her down the long passage, which resulted in my slipping on the mat and Sheila landing on top of me. Over tea and fruit jelly we decided that, though we were too old for these sorts of pranks, childhood games really were the best.

We drove to Batu Sapi and sat watching flying fish and a swift feeding its young in a nest in the wall of rock. We told each other about our childhoods and our hopes for the future.

'You're in love, aren't you, Wendy?' Sheila said to me.

'I don't know. Maybe. Probably.'

'Just be careful. Be sensible – like you are in other areas of your life.'

Easter Day began with breakfast and a picnic on Berhala Island with Mr and Mrs Meyer. This tranquil place had once been a leper colony and had interned both civilians and PoWs during the war. The day ended with the baptism of my godson, Cedric Ticobay, and before I knew it I was back in Tongud. I found people from the kampongs busy repairing the tamu houses. Joan and John had returned with the ponies and I watched Ederiss and young John, the brother of Helena, jumping from one to another on the *padang* (playing field). It looked like a dangerous pastime to me, and I hoped I wasn't going to be dealing with lots of broken bones. The boys, who had never seen a horse before, appeared to have no fear, which worried me even more. Many of the locals thought they were cows – which they also had never seen!

When we got chance to sit down and talk properly, I couldn't keep it to myself, and told Joan all about Rob and me. John burst in on us and, slightly reluctantly, I poured it all out to him too.

'He wants me to go and live in New Zealand with him. A new start for us both.'

Joan's eyes were like saucers. 'Will you go?'

'I don't know.'

Frank said that Dr Galea, the new doctor in Sandakan, would not be coming to Tamu. This was disappointing news. I had asked numerous patients – those with puzzling cases, or things I simply preferred to leave to a qualified doctor – to come to see the medical officer when he visited us for the festival.

Even though, with our unreliable radio, I wasn't sure if Frank could hear my reply, I had to say something.

'Do you realize, Frank, that no doctor has been to Tongud since Dr Christiansen two years ago? What sort of message does that give everyone?'

I was fuming as I dashed back to the house, where John Goodricke was about to start supervising the boys as they replaced our atap roof with an aluminium one. Joan and I cleared the rooms and covered everything with dust sheets. Always quick to spot my moods, Joan asked what was bothering me. After I had told her, she thought for a while. Then she said she knew that it wasn't right, but that my own competence might be at the root of it all, and that if I hadn't proved myself to be so capable I might have been given more assistance, which ended up making me even more annoyed!

The roof was a long, slow job. The supporting poles had to be tied together with rotan, which needed to be split first. The boys worked until it was dark, and started again at dawn. The next day they needed to fetch more wood, which had to be stripped of bark first. Lily and the girls came to help Joan and me clean up when they had finished. We had to sweep the beams, the walls and the floor and then wash everything down. I gave them some material and a box of coloured crayons to thank them.

The post arrived, including something from New Zealand.

'Is it a fat one?' I asked, unable to hide my excitement.

'What do you expect to find in it – an engagement ring?' joked John.

I managed to read it in the afternoon when the dispensary was closed. Rob said he had nothing particular to say; he just wanted to cheer me up. He was in Wellington, which he found to be a pleasant town: small and not crowded, with timber houses as well as more modern blocks. The weather was mild, though he had seen snow on the Southern Alps in the distance as he had flown into the city. I smiled when I

read about his pleasure in staying fresh after his evening bath
– we all knew that this was impossible here in the tropics –
and of sleeping snugly under his blankets. He knew only too
well how I longed to return to a temperate climate. He also
spoke of the strong affinity he had felt with me from our first
meeting – almost as if we were related, he said – and how, to
his surprise, it had quickly changed to deeper feelings. Now
he wanted only to spend the rest of his life with me.

I reread the letter several times that afternoon, and again
in bed that night. He was right – I had been feeling rather
low, allowing my worries to get on top of me. It was uncanny
the way he could guess my feelings from all those miles away.
The letter was just what I needed to lift my spirits.

Tamu (the festival) meant guests, who this year included
Father Stally, an Indian vet called Mr Rajah, agricultural
officer Mr Chong, and John Iceton, who was a dentist.
Dressers came from Lamag and Penungah to help Samuel
and me in the dispensary. As promised, the Resident and
Mrs Wookey arrived in their speedboat. We put some of our
visitors up at the kedai, and others in the dispensary and in
Arnold's new house, which the boys and villagers had been
working flat out to finish.

Arthur Stally brought with him something we had been
waiting for for a long time.

'They finally released it from customs when Frank had
enough funds to pay the duty. I hope it's worth the wait.'

It was the new tele-radio.

I missed some of the entertainment the locals were putting
on as I was so busy looking after our guests. There were 13 to
cook for, though I had a break one lunchtime when we were

invited for a meal at the kedai, provided by the Panglima and all the OTs.

The Tongud school concert took place in the valley this time, the audience sitting on the sides of the hill. Then we all went down to the berunsai and I drank some rice tapai with OT Harun and Mr Wookey. Ederiss got me on my feet to dance, but I made an exit as soon as I felt it was seemly to do so as I had reports to write and letters to send to Sandakan with the returning guests the following day.

As always after Tamu, I felt as if I needed a holiday. When I realized that it would probably be my last, I felt relieved and also rather sad.

17

Wild horses

May to June 1962

I was terribly busy in the dispensary in the next few days. We still had visitors from the kampongs, and I was making the most of the opportunity to give them the cholera vaccine. Twice I had to send Samuel home because he was unwell, and I badly missed my assistant.

One afternoon a patient, Ramug, was brought from Menanon with an intestinal obstruction. He hadn't opened his bowels for eight days and I could feel a hard mass in his abdomen and a large swelling on his left side. He was in great pain and was sure he was going to die. A simple enema failed to produce anything except large amounts of mucus. I decided he must go to Sandakan as an emergency the next morning. We arranged for Simin and her father to go too – Simin for a check-up and her father for his swollen knee – as well as a man with a large growth on his spine. I saw them off on *Malaikat Raphael*; I would have liked to go with them but was too busy, so John agreed to accompany them, and Simon and a younger boy he was training went as skippers.

Three days later – a Sunday – I woke up with abdominal pains and some dysentery. I went back to bed after Mass and stayed there all day, sleeping and reading Tolstoy's *What*

I Believe. I made notes to share with Rob. No one came to bother me. In the late afternoon I ate a little of the summer pudding I had made the day before with tinned blackberries, but that was all I could face.

It was 6.30 p.m. and almost dark when two boys came into my room to say that there had been an accident, and Joan had been hurt by Angip, one of the four ponies. I pulled on a sarong and rushed out of the front door. Joan was being half-carried towards the dispensary by Arnold and one of the boys. She was covered with mud, her face deathly white, and she collapsed before we could put her on the bed. Her left wrist was hanging at an unnatural angle. In a tiny voice she managed to tell me that she had been inspecting old sores on Angip's back when he kicked her hard in the side, throwing her several yards and causing her to land heavily on her left arm.

I suspected fractured ribs as well as a broken wrist as she complained of severe pain in her right side and difficulty in breathing. After treating her for shock and giving her something for her pain, I went through my text books to try to work out how to treat her.

I was giving her a blanket bath when there was a great commotion outside and a man was carried into the dispensary with blood pouring from a foot injury. I had no choice but to leave Joan and attend to him. He had driven a small knife right through his foot, from one side to the other, near the ankle. There was no time to lose, and I had to set to and suture the wounds on each side. Arnold – so much braver these days! – held the foot while one of the man's companions held a pressure lamp so that I could see what I was doing. The man holding the lamp gasped at every stitch I made, causing the light to sway backward and forward. I had to ask him to hold it steady so that I could do my job. When I had finished stitching I applied a dressing, gave him penicillin and Thiazamide tablets to take for several days, and instructed him to remain in Tongud until my return, for I had made up my mind to leave at 5.30 the next morning to take Joan to hospital.

I returned to my friend. I had all the mission staff with me now. Rosemary helped me to support Joan while I applied strips of Elastoplast over her right ribs. Then I began to prepare for a general anaesthetic. I asked Julius to squeeze her right upper arm to make the veins stand up and, miraculously, hit the vein at the first attempt. Joan counted to 17 before she was unconscious. I then got Arnold to pull on her left upper arm while I pulled on her hand to reduce the fracture. Everything went far better than I could have dared to expect, and I felt fairly confident that the arm had gone into a good shape, though only an X-ray would show the true result. Julius held her arm in position while I applied a back splint of plaster of Paris and used a gauze bandage to cover it.

Joan was starting to regain consciousness just as we finished and couldn't believe it was all over. She said her wrist already felt much more comfortable.

As *Malaikat Raphael* had not yet returned from Sandakan, we had no option but to set sail in an open perhau. I felt a small lump in my throat as, in the early morning mist, I watched Joan being carried by the boys on a home-made stretcher, down the hill to the river, covered in a coloured blanket of knitted woollen squares. There was something very poignant about that scene: was it the helplessness of my friend, a person who never made a fuss about her own ailments? Or was it that cheerful blanket, made as it had been by well-wishers at home who could never know how useful their gifts would turn out to be?

After a short heavy shower it became unbearably hot and sunny. At Bangan Camp I went to see the manager to ask if he could help us get to Sandakan more quickly. He agreed to lend us their speedboat to get to Lamag, where I hoped we would be able to pick up another. The stretcher only just fitted inside. We travelled quickly, though rather unnervingly, the driver constantly swerving to avoid logs in the river. I squatted beside Joan. She was very woozy, and for much of the time seemed unaware where she was and what was happening.

We reached Lamag at 3.30 p.m. to find the survey launches *Gillian*, *Zoe* and *Otter* all there. Peter Warner was with the ADO and said he was leaving for Sandakan the next morning in *Gillian* and that we could go with him. There was little point in going sooner as we wouldn't get far before dark. The Ibans who worked for Peter carried Joan's stretcher up to the ADO's house. That evening she passed water for the first time since the accident, and to my horror I saw that it was bloodstained. I gave her pethidine tablets for the pain in her side and tried not to worry too much.

Joan slept for most of the journey to Sandakan, where we arrived in the early afternoon. While we were waiting on the boat for Dr Galea to send an ambulance, Joan asked for the bedpan. Being desperate myself I used the female urinal, under my sarong, despite there being people all over the wharf and bobbing beside us on the water. Nothing like an emergency, I mused, for making you lose your inhibitions! I then had to quickly empty them both over the side of the boat and rinse them out.

Once we were in hospital Joan was swiftly X-rayed. She had broken her radius and two ribs, one of them in two places. Dr Galea came to speak to us and said that Dr Fozdar, the surgeon, would treat her the next morning. Once I was happy about leaving her, I went to St Monica's. I was relaxing in the bath when Mrs Wookey came round to find out what had happened.

I had just had breakfast the next morning when Arthur Stally appeared.

'News does travel fast!' I said.

Father Stally listened to the sorry tale, and said he would visit Joan later.

Back at the hospital I saw Joan and spoke to Dr Fozdar about her and my other patients. He said that the broken wrist was serious because the impact had affected the bone surfaces in the joint, which might lessen the chance of a full recovery. But I'd reduced it very well and he would only add more plaster around the arm, which I was pleased to hear. They would watch the urine carefully. He told me that Ramug, the patient I had sent a few days earlier with the abdominal obstruction, had had a gangrenous strangulated femoral hernia, and it was a miracle he survived.

By the time I had visited all my patients, the morning had gone, and I went back to the boarding house to have lunch with Sheila before having a rest. Later I went to the post office where there were some letters waiting, but none from Rob.

'What's all this about wild horses?' came a voice the next morning as I was washing the breakfast dishes.

It was Mrs Meyer, and we caught up with each other's news. Later, after visiting Joan and having lunch with Irene at the rectory, I went for the post and was happy to find a letter from Rob. He was still enjoying New Zealand, where he found everyone friendly, and he had made progress in looking for a job. He said if it worked out we would live in the countryside, probably moving every few years, which would allow us to see most of New Zealand before deciding where we would like to settle permanently. He ended the letter by telling me that he had booked a twin-berth cabin from the UK to New Zealand for March 1963, and wondered if I would like to go with him.

I read this a few times, my heart pounding. It shouldn't have come as a shock, when he had spoken already about us starting a new life together in this antipodean country, but it did. It began to sink in just how far away I would be going from my family and friends and all that was familiar to me if I were to accept his proposal.

I wrote a letter to Joan's parents, though I found it hard to concentrate, so I started one to Rob instead. I was glad to go to the cinema with Sheila: in the darkened auditorium it was easier to forget the rest of the world.

Joan was annoyed with herself over what had happened and for its impact on her pupils, as Arnold had decided the school would close early for the summer.

'You must be so angry with me,' she said tearfully from her hospital bed, 'wasting your time with me when—'

I interrupted her. 'Angry? Joan, in that instant you became my patient. These things happen. We can't control everything.'

'Angip was the nerviest pony on the journey,' she went on. 'I should have been more careful. But he had every right to be jittery – the poor creature ended up in the water once, and another time, when the raft he and John were on hit a rock, he tried to jump out. It's not his fault.'

I tried to soothe her as I helped her with her lunch, and she became less agitated.

'Make the most of your stay here and being looked after,' I said as I got up to leave. 'You won't get this sort of treatment back in Tongud! And get better! I'll see you soon.'

Her eyes filled with tears when I kissed her goodbye.

I received reports on Joan's progress when I was back in Tongud. One day she was sitting in a chair; another day she was walking. When I found myself back in Sandakan with two emergency patients just over two weeks later, she was recuperating in the boarding house and gave me a lovely welcome. She asked what had happened to Angip, and I told her that someone downriver had offered to buy him, though John was wary of handling him.

'But no more accidents, I hope?'

I assured her that the pupils had been forbidden from going anywhere near him.

'On the way back to Tongud, Wendy, I want to stop and say thank you to all the people who helped us to get here. But my biggest thank you is to you. Look how well I can move my arm!'

Frank and I had a meeting at which we discussed finances – and Rob. I didn't know how it had happened, I told him, but we seemed to have skipped the boyfriend and girlfriend stage and had moved swiftly to becoming practically engaged. He listened sympathetically. I told him I wasn't sure what the future held, but that I would be finishing my posting in Tongud whatever happened.

Later, Peter Warner dropped by the boarding house, saying he'd hoped he would find me. Rob was flying back the next day and he could take me to meet him.

I felt sick with excitement and trepidation as Peter drove me to the airport in a Land Rover. Rob had a huge smile on his face when he saw me waiting.

'New Zealand clearly suits you,' said Peter, and we both agreed that he looked very fit and well.

We dropped in at their office, where Peter made us coffee, and then he drove us to the Sabah Hotel and left us there. Over dinner, Rob gave me a little brooch he had bought me, and a box made from New Zealand wood. He was full of enthusiasm for everything about the country.

'There are some odd customs, but on a second look they are perfectly sensible. Most places close on Saturdays and Sundays and it's hard to get a meal after seven! But these things wouldn't worry residents as much as visitors. You know, Wendy, I think we'd both fall on our feet there.'

After eating we took a taxi up to the Residency and walked to our favourite spot in the Chinese cemetery on the hilltop, where I had first gone with Lawrence.

I told Rob I had been overwhelmed by his letters, which had repeatedly told me how much he loved me.

'In my family we don't usually express our feelings,' Rob admitted as we looked down on Sandakan, the bay illuminated in the moonlight. 'But I'm going to be the first to change that. If I don't put things very well, be assured that it's lack of practice and not for want of feeling.'

I told him I was happy for him to practise on me.

One afternoon, Rob said he was sorry for the times he had teased or challenged me over my beliefs, and admitted that he had been deliberately provocative and did not necessarily believe everything he said.

'So come with Sheila and me this evening to see *St Francis of Assisi*,' I urged him.

He said no, he wouldn't enjoy it.

'Why not make up your mind after you've seen it?'

But he still refused.

We returned to town where we went our separate ways. Sheila and Sister Florence were leaving for the cinema as I got back, and we all found the film very moving and impressive. That night I kept thinking about Rob's refusal, and wondering if – when he hadn't even been prepared to humour me over a film – he could really be Mr Right.

18

Endings and beginnings

June to October 1962

Rob and I continued to see each other regularly, and to talk about everything. Perhaps we talked too much. Perhaps some of the things would have been better left unsaid and sorted out later in the course of our daily lives.

As he seemed proud of his well-connected family – whom he told me were listed in *Who's Who* – I told him one day that I was descended from the Greys of Northumberland.

'Earl Grey, the British prime minister?' he asked, sounding impressed. 'The man the tea is named after?'

'We have a statue of him in the centre of Newcastle,' I replied, before adding, 'Not directly from him, but the same family. But does that sort of thing really matter? Does it make you love me more?'

One day I told Rob I didn't think I could go to New Zealand with him so soon after my return to the UK, and possibly not at all. I wasn't sure if I wanted him to accept what I said or to try to change my mind. He did neither.

We returned to the boarding house for tea and took our leave on a somewhat cooler note. Sister Florence was back from Sapi, and that evening she and Sheila went to a meeting. I stayed in and gave way to misery.

But when I saw Rob the next day we made up our differences and I was happy again. I seemed to be bouncing from one extreme to the other.

I ended up staying longer in Sandakan than I had anticipated because I had been suffering from earache and was being treated by Dr Willis. When it didn't get better I went back to see Dr Sychta, the ENT specialist who had performed my tonsillectomy. He diagnosed a fungal infection and told me not to return to Tongud until it had cleared.

I returned to the boarding house where Sheila was listening to the radio in the kitchen.

'Sshh!' she said as I began to talk.

The presenter was telling how Bishop Wong had returned from a trip to the UK with money to buy a new radio for Tongud.

'The nurse, Miss Wendy Grey, who lives on the remote Mission of the Epiphany, once carried out an operation step by step following instructions given over the radio by a doctor in Sandakan. The plight of this nurse, who often trudges for miles on dangerous journeys to visit the sick, touched the hearts of a congregation in Taunton, England, and now she will be able to carry on with her vital work.'

'I feel as if there should be violins playing,' said Sheila, laughing.

'Goodness, me too! Of course it wasn't quite like that, Sheila. The radio was nowhere near the dispensary, but it does sound even more dramatic the way they tell it!'

I knew that Rob was due to go away for work but I had expected him to come to say goodbye. When I hadn't seen him for a few days I drove to his office, where the old Iban told me he had left two days earlier and would be back in about a month's time. It was an awful shock. I managed to thank him and stay composed, but as soon as I was in the car the tears flowed and wouldn't stop. Back in the boarding house, I lay sobbing on the bed until Sheila came in and talked with me to calm me down.

The next few days were a busy time, which kept me from dwelling too much on my confused feelings. Frank had a visitor and invited Joan and me to join them on Berhala Island, where Frank, Majang and I had great fun playing with an enormous log in the sea and trying to push each other off it. Joan laughed at us from the safety of the shore. On the way back we saw scores of huge pink and purple jellyfish in the water.

Bishop Nigel and Mrs Cornwall arrived for a farewell visit. The diocese of Borneo was splitting into two bishoprics: Kuching and Jesselton. Bishop Nigel would be returning shortly to the UK and Bishop Wong would become bishop of the new diocese of Jesselton, and thus be responsible for those of us in North Borneo. St Michael's Church hosted a Chinese makan for Bishop Nigel at the rectory, and there were speeches afterwards. When the Cornwalls left, the mission staff and most of the congregation went to the wharf and gave three cheers as the boat steamed off.

Joan had made an excellent recovery.

'Have you met my orthopaedic surgeon?' she would say to people when we were together.

I had to admit that even I was rather impressed with the job I had done!

Joan, Arnold and I attended the diocesan division in Jesselton in July. The church was packed for the inauguration of the diocese of Jesselton and the enthronement of our friend Bishop Wong. Peggy, in a scarlet gown, led the way as the dignitaries processed into church. The police band blasted out a fanfare of trumpets. We took photos and there were refreshments after the service. In the evening, more than 150 guests attended a ten-course Chinese banquet at the Jesselton Hotel.

There was little time to be alone amid the celebrations, and then the short retreat for the mission staff, but one evening I managed to walk along the beach and sit and watch the sunset before supper. It was a good time to think about Rob and everything that had happened between us. My heart was telling me that I loved him – though probably not as much as he loved me – while my head was reminding me of the differences in our beliefs. Later – with great sadness – I wrote a letter telling him that, having given the matter much thought, I believed we were not right for each other. Knowing how distressed he would be, I said how sorry I was for shattering all his hopes and dreams, and hoped he could forgive me.

Back in Tongud I didn't like the look of Jeremy, who was shaking a great deal. I treated him as best I could, but feared there was little I could do.

One morning he crawled on to my legs as I ate breakfast in bed, and lay there heavily. He showed no inclination to move when I got up, so I disentangled myself as gently as I could. When I returned to my room later that morning he was still there. I went to stroke him and realized he was no longer breathing. My tough little cat – not old in cat years but a veteran of jungle life – had died. Joan and I buried him just beyond the kampong in a spot where he had sometimes liked to lie. In some ways it was a relief that I wasn't going to have to leave him behind when the time came for me to go.

On the way back from the burial we saw Mr Roberts, the ADO, who had stopped on his way to Penungah. He was talking to a group of men outside the kedai, including the OT and the Towkay. He winked and nudged me, and told the others that I was returning to England in October to be married. They all looked so pleased and interested and not at all surprised. I suppose it was the most natural thing in the world from their point of view and, if anything, I was more unusual in being 32 years old and a single woman! I didn't have the heart to tell them that I didn't think it was going to happen.

Malaikat Raphael, with Simon at the helm, had gone to meet Frank and Bishop Wong, who were coming to Tongud for a confirmation. When I heard the engine I went to greet our visitors.

'*Malaikat Raphael* is the smartest boat on the river,' declared the bishop as he disembarked.

I looked at my assistant. 'Did you hear that, Samuel?'

Samuel, who was standing a short distance away, beamed. On an unusually quiet day he had painted our restored jungkung white with a pale blue band. The crew now wore a uniform of navy shorts, white shirts and peaked caps.

Frank brought letters and I saw that there was one from Rob, which I decided to read later. I had made peace with my decision and didn't want his reply to upset my mood, especially when I had guests to look after.

I had a long talk with Frank and Bishop Wong about my future. I told them that though I had had the most amazing experience of my life so far, I couldn't cope with another tour in this climate. I hoped that the SPG would be able to use me elsewhere, in a more temperate climate. The bishop accepted my decision without question, saying that he expected the Peace Corps nurse to stay for two years, but he would also appeal to the SPG for another nurse.

Only half of the expected 102 candidates turned up for the confirmation service the following day, because of the flooded rivers. A couple of nights earlier John had dashed in as Joan and I were preparing a meal to tell us that the dam he had been building was in danger of being swept away. He had taken some boys with him to try to save it, and thankfully, three hours later, had returned, bedraggled but successful.

Frank preached in Malay, and his message was simultaneously translated into Dusun. Despite the reduced numbers, the building was packed; toddlers and dogs ran around, and children removed their clothes to feel more comfortable.

Afterwards Frank and I sat and had a beer together from the dispensary fridge. I told him more about Rob, and how in the letter I had just received he had told me how sorry he was about my decision as he was convinced that I was the love of his life.

'I feel terribly guilty now,' I told Frank. 'I feel as if I've upset his life as well as hurting myself. Oh, what a mess I'm in!'

Frank took my hand. 'Things will become clearer once you're home, Wendy. If you're meant to be together, it won't be impossible for you to meet again. For now, make the most of your last few weeks in Tongud.'

I packed up all my heavy belongings and took them to Sandakan to be shipped home ahead of me. I was also going to meet and bring back the Peace Corps nurse who would be my replacement.

Gay was slim, smartly dressed and friendly. I couldn't help thinking that she seemed very much a city girl. Could someone like her settle somewhere like Tongud? But it seemed unfair to make assumptions so soon. Wasn't I a city girl too? For all I knew, people might have thought the same of me. We spent a long time talking and I gave her a list of things she might need to bring to the mission.

One afternoon I took Gay and another Peace Corps volunteer, Mary, to see the film *Spanish Main*, after which we went to the Sabah Hotel for dinner. It was such a shock to bump into Rob in the entrance. He was with Peter Warner and two other colleagues. He was polite and friendly and gave no indication of the hurt I had caused him. I introduced my companions to him and we all chatted, after which he sat with his party and I sat with mine. The meal was good and I enjoyed the company, but I was only too aware of Rob and his friends at the next table. I could feel something like a current between us; it was so powerful it was hard to believe that Gay and Mary weren't aware of it. After driving them back to where they were staying I felt depressed and lonely. I wished I had invited Rob and his friends to join us. I wished I had been friendlier and asked him more questions about how he was and where he had been. But it was all too late now.

It was hard to think of anything else on the voyage back to Tongud the following day.

'I'm gonna wash that man right outa my hair!' – Wendy and Gay at the bathing spot

Gay and I were both feverish when we got back. I rigged up a mosquito net for her over the camp bed in my room. I kept her in bed for two days. Then, when she felt fitter, it was a luxury to be able to stay in bed myself and leave the dispensary to her. I took her to meet the pupils, and we went for a walk around the kampong to introduce her to everyone. We stopped at the kedai and talked to the Towkay and the Panglima.

One afternoon we went to see an explosion of dynamite at the dam. The detonators – which couldn't be dropped or knocked – had been kept in Joan's cupboard for safety, and the dynamite had stayed in a box under John's bed! Any not required was supposed to be returned to the police magazine in Sandakan.

Arnold was in Sandakan where Rosemary had just given birth to their daughter, Grace, so it was just Samuel, Gay and

Wendy walks across
a tree trunk to visit a
patient, while carriers
bring medicines in
bongans

me who set off with our carriers to hold some clinics. The
newly cut path we had been told about was non-existent
in places and we had to scramble along the sides of steep,
slippery hills. The ground was wet and there were a lot of
leeches. We had been going about 90 minutes when Gay fell
and cried out in agony. She had dislocated her left knee joint,
but as she moved it slipped back into place. She told me she
had a congenital tendency to dislocation of both knees, but
it hadn't happened for a few years. It gave us both a shock.
After a while she was able to get up and carry on walking
slowly, but clearly in discomfort.

My feet were hurting too. I had a large raw patch on a
heel where a blister had burst, and both of my big toes were
throbbing.

'Elephants!' cried Samuel suddenly, pointing to a series of
what looked to us like muddy puddles. Sure enough, they

were giant footprints, about 18 inches wide, which Samuel said were a day old.

I could see that Gay was struggling. She kept stopping to pick off leeches and I was starting to worry we might not reach our destination in daylight.

Our guides were going so quickly and at one point were so far ahead that they couldn't hear us when we shouted. We were quite frightened as we knew it would be dark soon. We caught up with them when they stopped and asked them not to leave us so far behind, whereupon they set off again almost as quickly. We hobbled along, doing our best to keep up, and reached Sesege just as the last hint of daylight left the sky.

Gay had begun to cry over a pain in her left eye. I looked but couldn't see anything. I left her to rest and went to bathe in the river. When I got back to the house where we were staying, the people were drinking tapai and playing gongs. By now Samuel was complaining of a headache and fever, and I decided that, as we were all a sorry crew, I would have to shorten our proposed trip. I decided we would trek to Malagatan Besar and Kuala Tunkabit and try to find a boat to paddle home down the Rivers Malagatan and Tongud.

The next day I made an eye pad for Gay and she said she felt better. We held a clinic in Sesege for 25 patients. In Malagatan Besar I was pleased to see Patrick, the boy who had been so ill with the oral abscess. He said he wanted to come back to school, having only completed Primary Three before his marriage. On hearing this, one of our carriers, a father of three children who said he thought he might be 18 but wasn't certain, said he would like to go to school too.

As we set off again I took off my shoes and walked barefoot. My big toenails were now navy blue and very painful whenever I stubbed them.

We came to a wide river and saw a boat on the shore. My hopes rose, but I was told that the owner lived too far back for us to return and obtain his permission to use it. By now I was so desperate to relieve my poor feet that I took off my shorts and my watch and lay down in the water in my knickers and cotton top. Ah, that felt good! I dunked my head and drank some water. I hoped the thin cottons clinging to my body weren't too revealing when I stood up again, but I was past caring. We carried on, hobbling with our sticks, until we reached a kampong on the River Malagatan in the early afternoon. We held a clinic and spent the night there.

The next day a man let us borrow his gobang, but it leaked badly and Samuel spent a lot of time baling out.

I wondered what Gay was making of all this. It wasn't the easiest introduction to her new life, but was there ever one? I thought back to my own initiation with Gwynnedd and knew that while it had been different from this one, it had been no more straightforward, and probably more dangerous. I hoped for Gay's sake and for the people I had come to love so dearly that Gay was made of the right stuff for this job.

We travelled through two kampongs and held clinics in them both. It was dark before we finished the last one and the people lit a fire using damar to give us some light. I could barely conceal my glee when the OT said he could lend us a good perhau to complete our journey the next morning.

When we reached the River Tongud we found it flooded. The current swept us down quickly and we were back in Tongud at midday. Gay and I retired to bed early that night.

Whenever I got some spare moments I was packing my belongings and giving away what I thought might be useful to others. I gave clothes to Lily and the girls and I gave Samuel my record player and tape recorder.

Samuel was building another new house which he wanted to show me before I left, so after closing the dispensary for the morning we set off along the path. As we were walking, he told me he'd been crying the night before while he'd been thinking about my departure. I admitted that I had done the same thing myself while I was writing a card for him.

His house stood on a hill, benefiting from the breezes and a view of the river. It was about the same size as ours, or would be when it was complete. He was waiting for planks to finish the floor, then he would put up bark walls and make a table, which he said Fadder could use for services if he wanted. A live squirrel he had caught was hanging by its neck, to be eaten later. However, when Samuel removed the rotan to show me the animal, it took a mighty leap out of his hands, through the window and to freedom. Despite the loss of his dinner, neither of us could help laughing.

I left him to his rest and walked back in tears, thinking how much I was going to miss my loyal, funny assistant, who now felt like a friend.

The evening before my departure, Joan and I were invited to the boarding house for a meal. The desks had been pushed together to make a long table, and pressure lamps lit the room. Our names had been allocated to places around the table: mine was in the centre, with OTs from neighbouring kampongs on either side and OT Harun and Samuel opposite. We had beer and a meal of rice, chicken and vegetables.

Ederiss, who had organized the meal, made a speech in Malay, bidding me farewell. I got up and said some words in Malay, thanking them for the makan, and thanking all the OTs for coming. I said I was sad to be leaving as I had been very happy in Tongud, working in the dispensary, and had a good friend and attendant in Samuel. I made a joke about the weather, saying that three years of heat was hard for someone like me, coming from England, where it felt like being in the dispensary fridge. Then the OTs got up in turn and each made a speech, thanking me for what I had done, wishing me a long life and a safe journey to my kampong, and hoping I'd return and we would meet again.

We got soaked running over to the schoolroom, where Ederiss and another of the older boys had organized a show and concert, with all the pupils taking part. I didn't know whether to laugh or cry when I saw myself portrayed giving orders to a boy taking the part of Samuel, for they put so much effort into their sketches. At the end of the show, Joan presented me with a pencil drawing she had done of the mission buildings, signed by all the children. I was so touched I could hardly speak to thank them.

From there we went down to the large tamu building for the berunsai organized by OT Harun and Ederiss. Two large jars of tapai stood in the centre of the room and two smaller ones beside them. Ederiss offered me one of the small jars, and OT Harun said I must drink them both before they'd let me go home. I was almost ill at the sight of it, as tiny flies were crawling all over the tapioca on the surface. The gongs played as I drank, trying my best to hide my disgust. I said I'd have to have a rest and drink the other one later. Then the berunsai singing began. OT Harun called me back for more tapai, and we sat sipping our drinks in the centre while men and women, linking little fingers in a circle, slowly moved around us, wailing loudly. We joined in this dirge, which continued until after midnight. Then I thanked the

OT and left. I had September's monthly medical forms to fill in before going to bed.

I woke up feeling excited, sad and anxious all at the same time. I spoke by radio to Frank and joked that I was thinking of staying after all.

'Fine, Wendy, I'll cancel your passage,' he said, and admitted he was feeling the same about leaving Sandakan.

As I walked back to the house I stopped for a moment to gaze at my garden. It had won many admiring glances since Samuel had planted it for me. How lucky I had been to have a garden that was in bloom all year round!

I took a last look at some of the views that had become so familiar. In the valley behind our house, fruit was growing on the banks, and round the corner was wet black padi. Pigs snuffled happily in the mud, and a new run awaited our hen population, which had grown to 50. We were far more self-sufficient now than we had been on my arrival.

I spent most of the morning saying goodbye, and at 10 a.m. I made my way down to the kampong, accompanied by the schoolchildren, who were wearing red flowers and singing, 'Goodbye, Sister'. At the Panglima's house I couldn't speak for sobbing. I carried on to the kedai, shaking hands with everyone as I did my best to choke back the tears, which came in spasms. Lily, Helena and some of the women were crying, which only made me worse. Gay took photos of it all. As Arnold and I got into *Malaikat Raphael*, the children stood on the shore singing a song called 'Selamat jalan', which means 'goodbye'. Through my tears I called out, 'Selamat tinggal', which also means goodbye but is said by the person who is leaving.

Joan and I had said our goodbyes in the house.

'I'll miss our nightly chats and bathes,' Joan said. 'And hearing you say every time you get into the river, "This is the best part of the day!"' she added teasingly.

'Oh, Joan, thank you for all your help and support. I don't think I could have survived without you being here too,' I said. And I meant it. We had become part of each other's lives.

Now she stood on the shore with her brother, both of them wiping their eyes. We all waved and shouted until our boat had turned the corner out of sight. I continued to weep for ages.

Arthur Stally collected Arnold and me in Sandakan and took us to the new mission flat. Irene had had to fly home earlier because of the sudden death of her mother, so she missed the tea party Frank threw for me. There were about 20 guests, including the mission committee, the Meyers, Rosemary and baby Grace, and various Sandakan friends. Afterwards Frank made a speech and presented me with a cheque for $110. It was all completely unexpected.

Though we were flying home from Jesselton together, Frank was leaving Sandakan before me. Two busloads from St Michael's Church were at the airport to see him off, along with pupils from St Michael's and St Monica's schools, so it was a crush both inside and outside the building. Frank shook hands with everyone, which took ages. He was given so many gifts I wondered how he was going to carry them all. After he had left I went to visit my patients in the hospitals and to say goodbye to Dr and Mrs Willis.

I woke early to hear Sister Florence warning me that there was a swarm of bees outside and not to put the light on, so I crept around in the dark to get washed and dressed. She was going to Tongud with Arnold, so I drove them and Majang to the wharf to board *Malaikat*. It was still dark when we got there.

Sister Florence embraced me and said that she knew God would continue to guide me. Arnold and I stood facing each other, knowing that this was going to be our last meeting for a long time. He and Frank had changed my life, but how to put such thoughts into words? Arnold said he would miss me very much. I was determined not to cry again, but my voice faltered when I thanked him for everything he had done.

'I'm so glad I answered your call,' I said. After that I couldn't trust myself to speak.

Back at the flat I finished packing and made a tape recording for Samuel. Thoughts of the previous night, when I had been taken out to dinner by all my Sandakan friends, kept popping into my head and making me smile.

Arthur and Ann Stally took me to the airport, where Sheila, John Brummell and Dorothy Meyer were waiting. It was hard saying goodbye, especially as I had no idea if I would ever meet these friends again.

I had gained permission from the agricultural department to take some orchids home, and Dorothy had picked some from her garden the previous evening. In my handbag, with my tickets and passport, I also carried a dead scorpion and centipede, preserved in surgical spirit.

I wrote to Joan and Gay on the 80-minute flight to Jesselton. When I arrived, Miss Waites, Bishop and Mrs Wong and Dr Christiansen were at the airport, and whisked me off to lunch, where the party included other Jesselton friends and Frank. I had said so many goodbyes, and felt my heart break a little with each one, that it was a relief when a few hours later he and I were finally on the plane.

After stops in Kuching and Singapore we began the long flight back to London. We had seats together and talked for a while, but when I was offered the chance to move to three empty seats so that I could stretch out and sleep, I jumped at the chance.

Before I settled down I looked out of the window. All I could see now was water. The islands of south-east Asia were already behind us. I thought of everything I was leaving: of the people whose paths had crossed mine during my three years in Borneo, of the good times and the bad. I smiled at the memories. But it was time to go home.

Afterword

Leaving Tongud was one of the hardest things I ever did. I learned so much there. I loved the work and I loved the people. The trust, simplicity, hospitality, generosity and appreciation of the Dusuns would stay with me for the rest of my life.

But after spending three years in the tropical climate, I knew I could not go back to work there. On the long flight home, I wondered where I might go next. I had heard of 'caravan missions' in Canada, and wondered if they were a possibility.

I arrived back in London to be met at the airport by my aunt Rhoda, with whom I stayed for a night before returning to Newcastle. I recorded in my diary that she took me to a West End show, but I have no recollection of it! I think I was probably too exhausted to enjoy it.

I received a warm welcome at home in Northumberland. My father was then vicar of Healey, a tiny rural parish, and there I spent ten days recuperating, enjoying the peace and tranquillity.

What a relief to return to the cool English climate! Even the cold north-east winds of Northumberland felt welcome, and I can honestly say that I have never complained about the British weather since!

Ten days later it was a joy to return to see everyone at my old church, St George's, Jesmond, on the edge of Newcastle. My vicar and his wife, Graham and Olive Piercy – who were among the dozens of people to whom I wrote while I was in Borneo – asked me to join their family tea party that Sunday.

I was introduced to their curate, who had arrived soon after my departure and was due to move on.

Colin Rogerson – at 32, the same age as me – was tall, dark and handsome. Two days after our meeting I received a postcard from him asking if I would like to go to a play at the Theatre Royal the following Friday. He was on his way to a retreat at Kelham Theological College, and asked me to reply there.

And so we had our first date. As Colin saw me home on the train to Riding Mill I had the feeling that here was Mr Right! Courting soon led to engagement, and then marriage in February 1963 in St George's Church. We had a long, cold winter that year, and the snow was so deep on our wedding day that my parents were unable to return to Healey for three days.

We began our married life in Wooler in Northumberland, on the edge of the Cheviot Hills, where Colin served as vicar of Branxton and Ilderton, and where our daughters, Catherine and Jane, were born in 1963 and 1966.

I continued to think about Tongud, and to give talks about my work there. I received letters from Samuel and some of the schoolboys, begging me to return, which was both heartbreaking and very flattering. And I kept in touch with the two men who were responsible for my being in Tongud in the first place. Frank Lomax (who died in 2007) spent ten years as vicar of Prudhoe in Northumberland before returning to the Far East, where he became Vicar of Singapore Cathedral until his retirement. Arnold (who died in 2004) later served in Penungah and became Archdeacon Emeritus in 1991. He retired to Jesselton (now known as Kota Kinabalu). He and Rosemary visited Colin and me in our

Rosemary and
Arnold Puntang
visit Wendy in
Durham in 1991

parish in Durham, as did Val and Angelita Ticobay. Father
Ticobay eventually became Prime Bishop of the Episcopal
Church in the Philippines.

I would also meet again some of the sisters who had
become so dear to me, as well as Sheila Merryweather (who
later became Sister Sheila Julian), Miss Waites, and nurses
Beryl and Gwynnedd, the latter whom I used to visit regularly
when she returned to the UK. I even remember having a
quick meeting with Lawrence – and his wife! – when they
were passing through the North-East.

Sadly, Joan and I did not meet again. She carried on with
her missionary work and teaching, and died in 1997. I was
happy to discover recently that in the Anglican parish of
Brighton, Tasmania – where her loss is still felt keenly by
those who knew and loved her – a hall attached to her home
church has been named the Joan Goodricke Centre.

In 1975, I learned that a boat for the Anglican mission of Kuching, the *Elsie Stephenson*, had been named after my old friend and mentor, eight years after her premature death at the age of 51.

In 1985 I returned to Borneo with my daughter Catherine and spent three full and exciting weeks there, moving frequently between town and interior mission centres, meeting old friends and making new ones. The journey upriver from Sandakan to Tongud that had sometimes taken us six days now took eight hours, bumping along logging tracks!

I was happy to see that the church had finally been built, and there Majang – the former boatman – and one of the girls arranged a wonderful welcome tea for us.

As former patients heard about our arrival, they came to see me, some of them travelling for many miles on foot. Catherine said how strange it was to hear me speaking another language – Malay – for the first time. She got even more of a shock when one of the men lifted his shirt to show the scars of an operation I had performed to save his life! I also had the joy of being reunited with Lily and Samuel.

I returned to Borneo again in 2003 with my younger daughter, Jane. In Tongud I was moved to see the grave of Bruce Sandilands in a quiet spot down the hillside from the church, as I knew he had expressed a wish to be buried at the mission. Bruce had visited Tongud regularly but he had always made his own camp and provided for himself, not putting me or my team to any effort. He had died tragically in 1975 after falling ill on an expedition. In the diary found on him, one of his final entries said, 'If I die I have given my life to Survey for which I have always worked in

Wendy and Arnold meet Lily (holding Wendy's hand) and
her family in 2003

the belief my skills were best used that way to service of
God and fellow men.'

I attended a meeting in London in 2015 to end the Borneo
Mission Association (whose *Borneo Chronicle* had alerted
me to the need for a nurse in Tongud all those years ago),
and bumped into several old friends there, including Martin
Wilson, the young man who had been with the party on my
arrival in Tongud in April 1960. I also saw Sister Margaret
Lin-Din, who was with the CJGS in Sandakan, now renamed
the Community of the Good Shepherd and based in Kota
Kinabulu. I was overjoyed to meet the new Bishop of Sabah,
the Rt Revd Melter Jiki Tais, who is the first Dusun to hold
the post. To my astonishment, he had heard all about me!

Over the years, friends and family have urged me to think about publishing my handwritten diaries. It seemed to me a daunting task. Two or three times I began planning the chapters, and I even made a start on chapter one, but I never got any further.

In 2017 I looked through them once more and showed them to Peter West, a friend from church, who was very enthusiastic about what he read. Soon after we were with our long-time friends Alder and Gwenda Gofton. Knowing that their daughter, Barbara, is the published author of several memoirs and diaries, I asked Gwenda if she thought Barbara might be able to help. Things began to happen quickly after that, and SPCK jumped at the opportunity to publish my story. The diaries I sweated away writing under an oil lamp every night have been turned into a compelling narrative by Barbara.

It has been an enormous pleasure to revisit my three years in Borneo – and often a huge surprise. So many things I had forgotten! I hope that they will be interesting and entertaining to other people.

It seems most fitting that SPCK – a partner of USPG, the organization that sent me to Borneo, and founded by the same man – should be publishing my story.

Wendy Grey Rogerson
Durham
June 2018

Glossary of Malay and Dusun words

amah	maid
atap	(palm-leaf) roofing
barang	belongings, luggage
berubat	traditional medicine
berunsai	celebration
bintang	star
bongan	conical basket of bark worn on the back
damar	a resin obtained from tapping the trees
Dayak	indigenous people of Borneo
Dusun	ethnic group of Sabah (N. Borneo), today combined with Kadazan group and known as Kadazan-Dusun
gobang	small boat/canoe, strong enough to support an outboard engine
Iban	ethnic division of Dayaks, formerly called Sea Dayak
jungkung	flat-bottomed canoe (used to transport patients)
kajang	palm-frond roofing, also used to line walls
kampong	village, homestead
kedai	shop/booth
malaikat	messenger, angel

makan	to eat (Wendy uses it to mean a meal)
mameow	medical witchcraft ritual
orang tua (OT)	headman
padang	playing field
panglima	tribal chief; military commander
pantang	prohibited thing
parang	sword, cleaver
perhau	tiny dugout canoe, usually paddled
tamu	guest, visitor
Tamu	annual market/festival that centred on Tongud
tapai	local alcoholic drink, brewed from tapioca root
towkay	boss

Boats used by Wendy

Bintang Epiphany   A canoe (gobang) with an outboard motor and palm-leaf roof, later replaced by *Malaikat Raphael* (see the photo on p. 58)

Malaikat   Medium-sized boat with an engine, a cabin and hold, useful for transporting goods and people, but impractical for shallower parts of the river (see the photo on p. 118)

Malaikat Raphael   A flat-bottomed canoe (jungkung) with an outboard motor and palm-leaf roof, suitable for carrying a patient on a stretcher. The 25 hp engine reduced the journey time between Tongud and Sandakan to two days when travelling downriver (see the photo on p. 118)

Acknowledgements

First, huge thanks to my husband Colin Rogerson, our daughters Catherine and Jane, and my brother Joe for all their encouragement, enthusiasm and suggestions over the years – as well as for their patience in waiting for this book to become a reality.

Thanks to Peter West, who, after reading part of my diary in 2017, became convinced that the story should be told, and was ready to help in any way.

Very special thanks to my team in Tongud – Joan, Andrew and Arnold. It was wonderful the way we bonded like a close-knit family, enjoying being together, with God's love and peace flowing between us. Special thanks to Samuel, for being not just an assistant but also a good friend, and to all my Dusun friends and patients for the trust they showed in me.

I remain very grateful to the Tongud 80 of St George's Church, Jesmond, for their constant prayers and regular donations towards medicine and equipment, and to all my other supporters while I was away.

I am also so thankful to:

- Bishop Yong Ping Chung (a Bishop of Sabah after I left Borneo), who has been so keen for me to write about my experiences;
- my Mothers' Union sisters and brothers for their prayers and encouragement. Special thanks to Doreen Bilton and later Dorothy Nicholas who were waiting to help me with their computer skills;

- my vicar Arun Arora, his wife Jo, and all the loving, caring and supportive family at St Nicholas' Church, Market Place, Durham;
- my Newcastle consultant, my GP, and all the doctors, nurses and staff in the Chastleton Medical Group, Durham, for helping me to manage my many medical challenges, and for their interest in hearing how I went from nurse to anaesthetist, surgeon and dentist in just a couple of weeks;
- the League of Charing Cross Hospital Nurses and Ruth Buckingham, its president;
- Audrey Alder (née Hawkes), for organizing reunions in London for those of us who trained together, all of whom have been urging me to write a book for many years;
- Ann Turnbull, Cross Net coordinator for the North and Scotland, bringing Stephanie, Jean, Lorraine and myself together;
- Northumbrian Centre of Prayer for Christian Healing, with Karen and David Vickers, Randolph and Jen Vickers, and Carol's word from the Lord confirming that the book should be written;
- Ron, for all his help with printing, and Alison Swarbrick, for helping me to use my iPad and for her continuing support;
- my weekly prayer group – Doreen Bennett, Betty Hutchinson and Dorothy Terry – for their constant, prayerful support and encouragement over very many years;
- countless people over the years who told me, 'You must write a book!'

Loving thanks to Nan Lovett and Margaret Burn (née Leybourne), my special friends for 77 years from the Duchess's School, Alnwick. Also to Valerie Steele, for supporting me since we met at SPG's College of the Ascension in 1958.

And thank you, of course, to SPG (now USPG) for sending and supporting me, especially Dr Veronica Thress.

Last but not least, thanks to my co-author Barbara, and to her parents, Alder and Gwenda Gofton. Gwenda, in particular, was instrumental in passing her own enthusiasm on to Barbara after reading the newsletters and newspaper cuttings that I left with her. I cannot thank Barbara enough for coming to the rescue and finally bringing all my hopes and intentions to reality. Her passion and excitement have been thrilling for me, as she brought my experiences to life. Furthermore, she has astounded me by discovering further information about some of my old friends on the internet! I have admired her emphasis on detail and accuracy.

Working together has been a tremendous privilege and joy for me, for which I thank her, and I thank the Lord for bringing us together.

Wendy Grey Rogerson

Dare I admit to feeling dubious when I was first told that Wendy would like my assistance, thinking that tales of life on a mission station might not be of interest in today's world? Of course, I quickly changed my mind when I started reading: a sharp lesson in not making judgements too quickly!

I first went to meet Alison Barr and Sam Richardson at SPCK to discuss possible future projects in 2014, the year that my book *Is the Vicar in, Pet?* came out, so it is lovely that the ideal opportunity for us to work together has finally come along. I would like to thank all of the team there, and especially Alison, for getting behind this book so quickly, and for their advice and support along the way.

A big thank you also to Claire Maxwell of Maxwell PR for her valuable assistance, and to writer and editor Nicki Copeland.

Thanks to my mother, Gwenda Gofton, and to my husband, Mike Fox, for reading the book and for their comments on it, and to my sons Joseph and Thomas who also gave editorial assistance. Mike also did the illustration at the front of the book.

I would also like to thank SPCK for making my job easier by arranging to have the 140,000 words of Wendy's handwritten diaries transcribed into a Word document. And to Geethik, the company in Madurai, India, who did the job so professionally – and astonishingly quickly!

Thank you to Martin Wilson, who generously spent time answering my questions about his time in Borneo; to the Sabah Society, who gave me access to an article written by Joan Goodricke in their 1962 journal; and to my local library in Crawley, West Sussex, for tracking down some reference material for me.

Of course, I must also thank Wendy for entrusting me with such precious material, and allowing me this privileged insight into her life, as well as access to some personal communications.

I'd also like to say my own thank you to all the people who enriched Wendy's life in Borneo, and who have enriched mine through reading about them – and to apologize to those I was not able to include in the story. A book of this length inevitably meant having to make some difficult editorial decisions.

As always, thanks to my amazing agent, Sallyanne Sweeney, and her colleagues at Mulcahy Associates.

Barbara Fox